WITHDRAWN

D0821246

DATE DUE

GAYLORD			PRINTED IN U.S.A.

CARSON CITY LIBRARY

ALL IN THE DAY'S
RIDING

ALL IN THE DAY'S
RIDING

BY

WILL JAMES

Illustrated by the Author

MOUNTAIN PRESS PUBLISHING COMPANY
Missoula, Montana
1998

Copyright © 1998
The Will James Art Company
Billings, Montana

First Printing, November 1998

Library of Congress Cataloging-in-Publication Data

James, Will, 1892-1942.
　　All in the day's riding / by Will James.
　　　　p.　　cm. — (Tumbleweed series)
　　Originally published: New York ; London : Scribner's Sons, 1933.
　　ISBN 0-87842-390-7 (alk. paper). — ISBN 0-87842-391-5 (alk. cloth).
　　1. Cowboys—West (U.S.)—Social life and customs. 2. Ranch life—West
(U.S.) 3. West (U.S.)—Social life and customs. 4. James, Will, 1892-1942.
I. Title.　　II. Series: James, Will, 1892-1942. Tumbleweed series.
F596.J22　　1998
813'.52—dc21　　　　　　　　　　　　　　　　　　　　　　　　98-39215
　　　　　　　　　　　　　　　　　　　　　　　　　　　　　　　　CIP

PRINTED IN THE U.S.A.

Mountain Press Publishing Company
P.O. Box 2399 • 1301 S. Third Street W.
Missoula, Montana 59806

TO MY FRIEND
EARL

WILL JAMES
'30

BOOKS BY WILL JAMES

Cowboys North and South, 1924

The Drifting Cowboy, 1925

Smoky, the Cowhorse, 1926

Cow Country, 1927

Sand, 1929

Lone Cowboy, 1930

Sun Up, 1931

Big–Enough, 1931

Uncle Bill, 1932

All in the Day's Riding, 1933

The Three Mustangeers, 1933

Home Ranch, 1935

Young Cowboy, 1935

In the Saddle with Uncle Bill, 1935

Scorpion, 1936

Cowboy in the Making, 1937

Flint Spears, 1938

Look-See with Uncle Bill, 1938

The Will James Cowboy Book, 1938

The Dark Horse, 1939

Horses I Have Known, 1940

My First Horse, 1940

The American Cowboy, 1942

Will James Book of Cowboy Stories, 1951

PUBLISHER'S NOTE

Will James's books represent an American treasure. His writings and drawings introduced generations of captivated readers to the lifestyle and spirit of the American cowboy and the West. Following James's death in 1942, the reputation of this remarkable artist and writer languished, and nearly all of his twenty-four books went out of print. But in recent years, interest in James's work has surged, due in part to the publication of several biographies and film documentaries, public exhibitions of James's art, and the formation of the Will James Society.

Now, in conjunction with the Will James Art Company of Billings, Montana, Mountain Press Publishing Company is reprinting each of Will James's classic books in handsome cloth and paperback editions. The new editions contain all the original artwork and text, feature an attractive new design, and are printed on acid-free paper to ensure many years of reading pleasure. They will be republished under the name the Tumbleweed Series.

The republication of Will James's books would not have been possible without the help and support of the many fans of Will James. Because all James's books and artwork remain under copyright protection, the Will James Art Company has been instrumental in providing the necessary permissions and furnishing artwork. Special care has been taken to keep each volume in the Tumbleweed Series faithful to the original vision of Will James.

Mountain Press is pleased to make Will James's books available again. Read and enjoy!

The Will James Society was formed in 1992 as a nonprofit organization dedicated to preserving the memory and works of Will James. The society is one of the primary catalysts behind a growing interest in not only Will James and his work, but also the life and heritage of the working cowboy. For more information on the society, contact:

Will James Society • c/o Will James Art Company
2237 Rosewyn Lane • Billings, Montana 59102

PREFACE

Since I been using my rope arm and hand on writing and drawing instead of making a loop and a throw I've experienced a lot of pleasures that I wouldn't of if I'd still be making my living in the saddle. Like for instance, in my stories I can go over the trails that if I wasn't writing I would never think of again. The writing brings 'em back to memory, I can feel the hot sun that beat down on them trails and the blizzards that sweep acrost 'em, and experience again what happened along 'em.

In my pictures I often draw some feller that I'd plum forgot about and the likeness makes me see him some more. The same with the horses, the brakes of some hills, the settings of cow camps, and all that goes with the cow country. The pleasure is great with things popping back to sight as I write or draw that way, for then I can feel the spurs on my boots wether they're on 'em or not, I can feel my horse under me and ride again with the many riders I knowed amongst the herds in the big country around, wether I'm working at home on the ranch or in a hotel of some city.

In this book is a variety of writings that tell of the cowboy's riggings, the cowboy today, and why the high heels, the big hat and such like, along with experiences in narrow escapes that's all in the day's riding. I'm not stretching the truth in none and all can be proved in most every day of the cowboy's life. Even the stories, they might sound like fiction but they're from facts. I can tell a lie with a grin while making a horse trade but I can't write fiction, and as far as my writing being in cowboy vernacular, as some say, it strikes me as being only as anybody would talk who got his raising and education out-side,and where university roofs is the sky and the floors prairie sod.

WILL JAMES

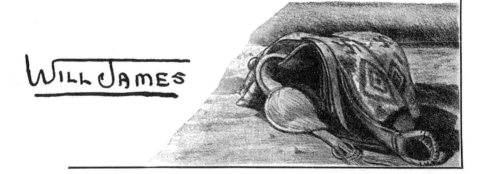

WILL JAMES

I didn't know that we
had vernaculars —

CONTENTS

ILLUSTRATIONS

ALL IN THE DAY'S RIDING

I

THE COWBOY TODAY

THE COWBOY TODAY

I'm thinking I've sure bit off a big chunk to chew on when I took it onto myself to tell some of the cowboy of to day because these cowboys of today, even tho they're the same as them of fifty years ago, are scattered over a powerful big territory, a bigger territory than the old time cowboy ever knowed.

To day you'll find the cowboy in Hollywood and doing work there with horse and rope that none other but a cowboy can do. The cowboy has been in Europe, and there to contest with others of his kind on bucking or rope horse for the prizes that was offered for the winner. He can be seen in such places as New York or Chicago and riding his bucking horse there the same as he does on the range, only he's riding in an arena and in front of a crowded grandstand. Last October the world's best riders, which comes only from the western part of the United States, when it comes to bronc riders, was gathered at New York for another big annual rodeo there.

But that ain't where you'll see all the cowboys of to day, not by a long shot. The good old range that once was stirred and tracked by big buffalo herds and ponies' hoofs has kept many spaces which are still sure enough wide and open. In them few spaces which scatters here and there along both sides of the Rockies and from Canada to Mexico you'll find the cowboy of today still doing pretty well the same work his old man has done.

1

The cowboy of today is still doing pretty well the same work his old man has done.

It's true of course that there's no more Indians that needs fighting, and that the longhorn cattle which was trailed from Texas to the Northern ranges has been replaced by the white-faced hereford, and even the long trails themselves are all cut up by strands of barb wire, but to the west of them trails is still a lot of open territory left where in some places the neighbors are some forty miles apart and no fences adjoining.

With the fine highways stringing acrost the big stretches and a powerful car to take a tourist along there's no chance much to see what there is of the west, but on both sides of them highways there's scopes of open range country, some of 'em a couple of hundred miles, in any way, which is still cowboy territory.

There the cowboy of to day is still as much of a cowboy as the generations before him ever was, and if anything more so, because he has the blood and backing of them generations, he inherited the pioneer edge to begin with and the first day of his life was with the surroundings that would make him nothing else but a cowboy.

His style might of changed some, but that even is for the better, his boots are of neater fit, his shaps are of better cut, his saddle more to fit him and the back of the horse it sets on. All in all the cowboy of to day is getting benefit from the experiences the cowboy of yesterday has went thru. With that and the skill that is bound to be inherited some, along with the spirit that goes with the making of a cowboy the young feller of to day, to my way of thinking, sure ought to be a thoroughbred.

Then there's the horses he rides. Civilization hasn't affected them ponies any, they're still wild, wild as any wild animal. The pure blood that's been throwed on the range to breed up the horse herds the last forty years or more hasn't at all took the buck and fight out of the original mustang that used to roam the plains, instead it's put hot blood in them ponies' veins, gave 'em more speed, strength, endurance, and the fighting ability went up till when to day you run in a bunch of range horses and pick out a few to break you sure find that it takes a A number 1 cowboy to qualify for the job.

Any good cowboy can still find plenty of that to do to day, and there's many a good cowboy still doing it with no thought for anything else, and why should he think of anything else? He's a cowboy and doing a cowboy's work. There's big scopes of country where he can ride his bronc without having to open a gate, there's plenty of good cattle and by the thousands on the ranges, and even tho these cattle of to day's might not wear as long a spread of horns as the old Texas cattle used to them horns are sure plenty long enough and it takes a pretty fair size loop to circle around some of 'em. What's more, them cattle are not at all of the kind that comes home every evening, they don't come home at all, winter nor summer, you've got to round 'em up when you want 'em and they're plenty wild enough. It takes a cowboy on a cowhorse to handle 'em, and that cowhorse can never be substituted by no machine, for them cattle have to be roped and branded the same as ever.

Maybe I'm a little stingy in telling of what all the West still has to make up the need and room for the cowboy. Like for instance, I can mention that there's still wild longhorned cattle and of the same breed that so many claim as being gone, they range like deer in rough countries and can only as a rule be got with a long shooting rifle, then there's the wild horses, hundreds of 'em right to day in near every state of the West, and if I'm any judge of horseflesh I'll swear that some of these ponies trace back to the original spanish horses.

Now, where there's wild horses, there's bound to be lots of room, more so where there's wild cattle, and when you take in some of

He's a cowboy and doing a cowboy's work.

today's cow outfits that's running ten and twenty thousand head of cattle that's bound to take *more* room, then there's the thousands of range horses that need a heap of room too (I'm not mentioning the sheep). So, take it any way you want you've got to allow that there *is* room, and there's where today's cowboy comes in, right in that roomy country of range cattle and wild horses, and no matter how many dams are built and how many irrigation ditches scar up the foothills the most of that country will stay as it is.

The cowboy's God has been good, he's saved him plenty of country that nobody can take away from him. It's too rough or dry to farm or irrigate and none of us alive to day will see the time when brogans will replace his riding boots or a shovel his loop.

A Cowboy To Be

I don't think I've ever flowered up any of my writings so as a feller would think the cowboy's life is easy, wild or romantic. I've done and I'm still doing my best to put it down as I've seen and lived it, and stuck as close to the facts as any feller can. There's no heros in my stories or articles, no fair heroines to be rescued from mad stampedes or villains, just plain everyday cowboy life, as plain and rough as the horses and the range country we live in.

And still, since I been writing such and got books published where I tell of the range life and of my experiences, there's many fellers been writing me saying how they sure want to come West and become cowboys, asking how they should start in and where to hit for. And when these fellers write and tell me they want to live such a life as I describe I kind of feel that they've got the makings of a cowboy in their backbone, and with a fair chance would turn out as such.

In my books I've repeated, *and I'll keep on repeating* that there's plenty of range land left, wide open stretches where you won't see a human for a year at a time. Of course there's no more free range, all is controlled by leases or water rights, but when you take a lease of one outfit that controls a hundred miles of range land at a stretch or water rights of another outfit that controls open country for a couple of hundred miles or more any way you go nobody can say there's no more room for the cowboy, for in such stretches is where the cowboy is needed to handle the thousands of cattle and horses that roam over the level and the rough of it.

As to where them stretches can be found, a feller can draw a line from West Texas on north to west North Dakota and every state west of that line can produce mighty open and wide stretches, stretches that a stranger would never dream is any more. The prairie is about gone to the farmer, but the mountains, the foothills, the rock-rimmed grass countries of the north, the badlands, the big deserts and the brush and the granite countries of the south where there's also plenty of feed still holds and, I figure, will hold for a long time over two thirds of the West. That's all cow and horse country.

It's easy to find any of them stretches, all a feller's got to do is just get off the railroads and highways once he gets West, and if he's not afraid to get lost he'll find himself by his lonesome a plenty before very long.

But hitting out on them stretches wouldn't be the way for a feller to start in getting a job as a cowboy, because no matter how much he's rode, how much he's practiced roping or how good a shot he is, if he's never done that in the western country he'll never get a job on an outfit, only maybe some job on the ranch but not on the range as a cowboy.

Even on the ranch they'll want experienced men and there's plenty of them out of work nowadays, and as far as getting a job as a range rider from the start that'd be plum impossible for a greenhorn, because there a greenhorn wouldn't only be in the way but what little he could do would be more harm than good and it'd have to be done over again. He'd do such things as bringing in the wrong bunch of cattle or horses, get bucked off or get lost and then the

In such stretches is where the cowboy is needed.

cowboys would be spending their time looking for him instead of doing their own work.

Fellers write and ask me to give them a chance and a job on my outfit, or let 'em know of some other outfit where they could get such. I have hundreds who ask me that, I'd like to help but I'm always full handed, I have experienced men and plenty more waiting in case I want to make a change. I have to have experienced men so everything can be done right and no loss come to the outfit and I know every other outfit is the same way.

I don't want to be discouraging, but I don't want to steer a feller wrong either and be blamed for it afterwards, and to be frank some more I don't think there's any harder game to break into than that of being a cowboy, and few games where there's less future, unless a feller saves his money and lines out on a little outfit of his own, as some cowboys do.

If a feller wants to be a cowboy I can tell of some way how he can try his hand and start in, but he don't want to expect to be one in a day or a year. First he ought to come West in early spring and not later than middle summer, then he ought to have enough money when he lands to hold him over till he gets a job, if he gets a job (jobs are scarce in this year of 1933) it ought to be on some farm that's always close to any town and where he'll get to learn a little something about horses and cattle, even if the horses are the work type and the cattle are for milking. In time he might get a job further out as a ranch hand on some small ranch where he might get to do some riding, such as bringing in the work horses and helping corral and brand stock once in a while. There he can learn some of the ways and lay of the country and from then on it's all up to him. If he's got the makings of a cowboy he'll find out of some open stretch where big outfits are running, with his wages he'll buy himself a couple of broncs to break and even though they might learn him more than he learns them that'll be a lesson he'll need to start with. By the time his horses are broke he'll also know something about a rope, by then he's also learned what kind of saddle, boots, spurs and general outfit he ought to buy.

All this he'll do while working as a ranch hand, and even tho he might be driving a team or shoveling out ditches during the day he'll have his evenings and Sundays for his riding and such like, and maybe the ranch owner will put him to riding more and more whenever the chances come.

A change of country is good for a feller that's learning, and soon as he's got his broncs broke well enough so they won't wear themselves out fighting instead of traveling he ought to hit out for new territory and another job on another small ranch. With his two horses he's pretty free and independent and he'll learn plenty more along the trail, but he hadn't ought to turn out as what we call a "grub line rider" (fellers that just ride from one place to another and take advantage of the hospitality of the country). Such fellers are looked down on by cowboys and cowmen.

Rambling thru the country a feller ought to have money enough to carry him in case he's charged for staying over night at some places. If there's no work at the outfits he strikes he hadn't ought to stick around, even if he's asked. But he ought to stop some place before his horses get too tired or thin and let them recuperate, even if he has to take a job he don't like and work for nothing, because the folks of the cow country sure don't think much of a man that's riding a tired and poor horse, and it'd be just as hard for such a man to get a job on the range as it would be for a ragged hobo to get one in some high office.

With two horses, one for saddle and one for pack, a feller can stop most any place, where there's good grass and water and let his horses rest. Going thru the country a feller ought to have two horses that way, then he can take a good roll of bedding along on the extra horse and the little necessary grub to do him when he camps out.

In this same book I have an article called "Thirty Years' Gathering" that describes what all goes to make up a cowboy's bed, and with such like a feller is pretty well independent as to where and when to stop, most any time of the year.

There's many more things I could tell on how a feller can start to be a cowboy, such as how much he'd have to pay for a horse, how to break him, what kind of saddle and rope to get and so on, but there's no need for me to go into that. If a feller has it in his heart to play that game I've given all the information that's necessary, to just come West and start in, as I said, the rest will come thru experience and that'll be a heap better and more than whatever I could tell by writing.

THE RANGE BLACKSMITH

The cowboy is his own blacksmith. He sometimes forges his own spurs and bits or branding iron, but he's best at horse shoeing and he learns to do that as well or better than any town horseshoer, because the cowboy is the one who rides the horses he nails the shoes on, and he learns mighty well how a shoe should be fitted by doing that riding.

On an average outfit the cowboy gets from eight to twelve head of horses in his string. All depends on the country and horses how many he gets. In the rocky and lava countries of the south, which stays rocky in many places as far north as the Montana line, the cowboy has to keep his whole string shod all the time. And even

With one foot tied up—

after a saddle horse is turned loose and there's no more work for him for a spell, if that horse is expected to keep in good shape while rustling feed over the rocky ground, he's often turned loose with new shoes on him.

In some of the lava countries I've seen shoes wear plum off a horse's feet within a month, while that horse was doing nothing but running free, hunting feed and travelling the long distances that layed between the water and that feed.

It was in such a country that one of my horses lost a shoe once. I rode him on for half a day, and he was limping bad when I run acrost the scattered parts of a prospector's shack. There I found a heavy horse shoe that must of belonged to some freighter's horse. It was away too big for my horse, and there was big toe-and-heel calks on it. But it looked good to me, and now the next thing was to shape it to fit some and find something to fasten it on with. Well, I shaped it with a rock, and finding a few rusty shingle nails amongst the scattered timbers of the shack I used them to fasten it on, with another rock for a hammer. It wasn't a very neat job, but it done fine for the time being, and my horse lost his limp.

Many of our horses don't take to getting shod. They'll fight and kick the shoe off when it's half on. Some have to be throwed and tied down, and it takes a range blacksmith to handle 'em, a cowboy.

"The Old Slicker"

The old slicker reminds me a lot of the old six-shooter. You can pack 'em both for three hundred and sixty-five days straight, and never need 'em; but lay 'em away for half a day, and you're going to get soaked to the bone, and meet a grizzly on your way back to camp.

I've wore out a heap more slickers by packing 'em on my saddle than I did on my shoulders. . . . We have a way of tying it back of the cantle so it hangs all on the left side and near drags the ground. That's done to sort of take the spooks out of unbroke horses, and make 'em used to things. A wild horse kicks at it and stampedes

To sort of take the spooks out of unbroken horses.

away, but pretty soon he gets used to it a-hanging there by his hind leg, and calms down to get used to other things that might spook him.

On horses that's hard to set, we sometimes tie the old slicker in front of the saddle to sort of have some chance with him. There's not so much swell-fork on our saddles, and on big tough horses, a feller has to have something to go by, so he can follow his horse in his winding jumps between the earth and the sky.

The old slicker does a cowboy a lot of good that way, besides being useful when the skies get cloudy and the rain pours down.

And if rain comes down heavy and a cowboy leaves his slicker in camp, he'll just cuss that slicker and use his horse for shelter, if his horse will let him. But for many uses, and if you're a wise cowboy, never leave your slicker in camp.

II

THE COWBOY'S WORK AND OUTFIT

THE BIG HAT

Maybe it's been noticed how, in the last year or two, the cow boys don't wear as big a hat as they used to. The first of that came to me while I was at one of the annual Chicago rodeos, and being it's at such events that styles are set, I got to wondering who or what was responsible for the change and the skimping on crown and brim.

I went on to other rodeos and noticed that the shrinkage in the size of the hat was pretty general. Of course it was still big enough for folks to notice, and the press cub could still describe it, in his very usual way, as a four or ten gallon hat, or as many gallons as he cared to make it.

But to me they looked small, and maybe that was on account that when I come to Chicago for the rodeo I was green from my home grounds, which is in a mighty open stretch of Southern Montana, and the boys there most all wore Stetson's top size.

I'd come from where we're a year or two behind in catching up on styles, and when I got to Soldier Field Arena, the change or shrinkage, even though it didn't average more than an inch to the brim, struck me sudden. There was only a half dozen riders there wore the big ones, and I was glad there was that many, because there's a whole lot to the feel and looks of that big hat and I'd sure hate to see it disappear.

I got to wondering on why the shrinkage in the man's-size hat that way, and figgered that maybe some top-hand cowboy had set the new style somewhere or other, which sometimes happens, and for no special reason—no more than when pants changed from peg top to balloon.

But I hope that style, or whatever it is, don't affect the big hat too much, because there's a powerful lot of use for it in its size which style shouldn't interfere with, and I don't think beaver hair ever was used to a better advantage than when it's turned out into the curved six-inch brim and seven-and-a-half-inch crown cowboy head-piece. That hat, costing from fifteen to fifty dollars, is one of the cowboy's pet possessions, and under it he feels a whole lot like he's riding in the shade of a juniper tree all the hot day long. The only time it comes off his head is when he crawls between his soogans to sleep, and even then it's the last thing to come off and the first thing put on as the cook hollers "Grub pile" at daybreak.

I hope that style, or whatever it is, don't affect the big hat too much.

The only time the big hat might be changed for some other head-piece is when the cowboy goes a traveling by rail from the home range to the rodeo grounds, or on other such rambles. He'll then most likely buy a cap and fit himself out to blend in with the folks around him, but while traveling that way—with a cap on his head—he'll have his hat in a bag close by, and when he gets to the other end and amongst his own, it won't take him long to make the change to his pet hat. The cap will go a sailing to a corner till he goes traveling again.

For in the rodeo grounds or on the range, the cowboy has a lot of use for that big hat. It comes in mighty nice to haze a bronc with, and in the wild-horse race at the rodeo you can see the cowboy turn his stampeding horse with a wave of it by his eye; a pull of the rein wouldn't mean anything with the wild pony. That goes for on the range, too, as there's where the cowboy has a heap more to do with the wild horse than just trying to make him win a race.

There's many other uses for that hat which comes in with the everyday work of the cowboy. Like, for instance, corraling a spooky bunch of stock; a wave of it at the end of a long arm will turn a bunch quitter and save a hard ride getting him back. A hard-shell derby would be sort of comical there.

Then again, the big hat goes mighty fine when a feller is riding a bucking horse, specially if that feller rides on skill and balance, and not on main strength. That hat in the rider's hand has the same use as the long stick has for the tight-rope walker, and if handled right, a lot of balance can be laid in there that is to the rider's advantage.

I found that out one day when I got bucked off in a catclaw bush, and I blamed my downfall to earth to losing my hat. I'd set my horse through what I claim was some pretty hard jumps, and I was getting onto the hang of him in good shape, when all at once my hat slipped out of my fingers. Well, after that I somehow couldn't keep track of my saddle no more. I felt like I figger a cat might feel if he went to turn a sharp corner at full speed and all at once lost his tail. Anyway I lost a considerable lot of balance when that hat slipped out of my fingers, and it wasn't long afterward when I took a "squatter's right" in the thick of the catclaw bush.

When I got on that horse again I took a firmer grip on the hat; he didn't get to throw me no second time.

There's a feeling that goes with them hats that's mighty dependable whether you have it on your head or in your hand. On your head, the low and wide-curved brim protects your eyes from the glare of the sun and keeps it from scorching your neck.

Both sides of the brim are trained to a curve, so that in a high wind the brim won't flap either up or down, for a cowboy often makes a breeze of his own when he's chasing a critter, and a flapping brim has a great way of coming down over a feller's eyes just about the time he's throwing his rope.

Then there's the high crown which keeps a good air space between the head and the top of the hat, and that helps considerable, specially when you're trailing a herd of tired stock acrost the hardpan flats of the desert. But you don't have to be out on the desert to find things hot; I've seen it mighty hot up on top of high timbered mountains at times, and I found that the high crown goes well wherever the sun shines.

So, all in all, whether the hat is on the head or in the hand, it sure has its use; besides what we call real style, also a heap of comfort. It sets on the head the same way a good old square-skirted double-rig saddle sets on a horse's back—and that's perfect. Another advantage in the good-grade big hat is that it's also light in weight—near as light as the little peanut of a hat the town man wears.

Not so many years ago, when the big hats growed to their biggest, I knowed a cowboy who wouldn't allow anybody to wear a bigger hat than he did. It was up in Oregon one day that he run acrost another cowboy who had him cheated by half an inch on the brim, and this feller does nothing but go up to him, measures his hat, and orders himself another a half an inch bigger.

I was with him when he received the hat, and even though it was some man's-size, I figgered it sure looked good on him, because that cowboy was some man's-size hisself. He knowed how to wear it and how to use it, and with it at the end of his long arm I expect he could of turned a blind bunch of wild elephants or hazed a bronc to committing suicide.

Pride has something to do with the cowboy wearing the big hat. It's part of what identifies him for what he is, what he's proud of being, but it's not for show that he wears it, because a feller don't have much chance to show off out there on the range, as there's nobody to look at him—only few of his kind who, regardless of what sort of a hat or rig he uses, would only laugh at him if he wasn't a real hand.

The cowboy is proud of his hat, but he'll use it for every need that comes along. The fine stuff that's in it is put together in a way that'll stand rough use, and when sometimes it's tramped on by hundreds of hoofs and mashed in the dirt, it's expected that the hat, after a little slapping against the shap leg, will be as good as ever, and it usually is.

Once in a while that same hat is throwed in a mad cow's face what's come to the rescue of the calf which the cowboy is branding. It most generally changes her course some, or at least makes her hesitate. Then again, while the cowboy is cutting out horses afoot in the corral, the big hat might come in mighty handy to send a-sailing and split the spooky bunch two ways.

There's many other ways where the big hat comes into play when it's not setting on the cowboy's head, and in it he's got something

Once in a while that same hat is throwed in a mad cow's face what's come to the rescue of her calf the cowboy is branding.

reliable and as useful as his spurs or rope or any part of his riggin'; also something he can be proud of, for the tall crown and the curved lines of the broad brim go mighty well with the slim length of the average cowboy as he sets his horse while working a herd, hazing mustangs or putting on action while in the middle of a hard-bucking bronc.

So, considering all, and how the big hat fits a cowboy's head and works so well, I don't think it'll go to shrinking much more than it has, and I hope it stays big, because the cow country is still mighty big and there's a lots of room and use for it.

"Thirty Years' Gathering"

"Thirty years' gathering" is what we call our bedroll out here on the range—the cowboy's bed—and "gathering" is a mighty fitting name, for the bedroll answers as a warehouse for all a cowboy might gather in his rambles. And when the cowboy crawls in between the soogans he's right amongst, and laying over and under, all he owns. All, excepting a couple of saddle horses and his saddle by the corral.

There's no taxes or overhead expenses worrying him as he goes to rest.

At the head of his bed is the war bag, a flour sack or some such like, which takes the place of a pillow. To make it soft or give it size, there's accumulated in there many things which is part of a cowboy's needs—tobacco sacks and cigarette papers, strips of buckskin and latigo leather to mend things with, some odd spurs, a marlinspike, and wrapped up with care might be the picture of some girl, a few frazzle-edged letters, and maybe some touchy poetry which has been tore out of old magazines. The cowboy might lay a coat over the war bag to make it extra soft, and if a spur rowel or something digs him in the ear, all he has to do is turn the bag over and pound it some. It's pretty well like finding the soft side of a boulder, but anyway, that's the cowboy's pillow, and he's glad to lay his head on it when night comes.

Under the war bag is a .30-.30 carbine or a six-shooter, or both. That don't help make the pillow soft either, but it seems like it's the only natural place to keep such when a cowboy is at home that way.

I knowed a feller once who'd replaced his war bag with a regular pillow—a real fancy one, but he hadn't been to blame for that—a young lady had sent it to him. She'd even put his first name on it with moonlight-colored threads and worked some more of the same in fancy braiding all around that pillow. It was sure a cute thing and us boys would take turn about keeping it perfumed by bringing wild flowers and scattering 'em around it. Of course we'd always be sure to do that when the privileged cowboy would be missing, 'cause he was sort of sensitive about that pillow, and the flowers we'd bring didn't always smell so good as some others. One time when the wagon was sent in for grub, a few of us chipped in and had a six-bit bottle of perfume brought out. We spilled the whole thing on the pillow at once and covered it up well, and a few months later, when

I left that outfit for other ranges, the pillow still smelled, and the cowboy who owned it was still sensitive about remarks on perfume and pink colors on sky-blue silk.

The other things that go to make an average cowboy's bed are the soogans—quilts. Two or three of them, folded double, take the place of a mattress, and they're better than a mattress because they can be took out easier and shook up and aired through; then again, among each fold of them quilts is a great place to lay clean clothes so they won't wrinkle. If a cowboy has a suit, he can lay it in there, and when shipping time comes and he goes to town, he's got a clean suit all nicely pressed to put on.

Shirts and underwear and socks are kept among the folds of the under soogans, too, and every kind of clothing he wears which he wants to keep clean and pressed.

As for the other part of the bed, a light double blanket is used to crawl in between, some heavier ones on top, and maybe a soogan. That all depends on what the weather hands out. The whole bed is inside a long waterproof canvas called tarpaulin, or tarp for short. The tarp, which is about seven feet wide by sixteen feet long, folds over the whole thing and snaps on top so no cold winds or snow or dust can get in the bed.

At the foot of the bed and on both sides between the bedding and the tarp is another handy place to keep things in, such as an extra pair of boots, the pet rope, a spare cinch, clothes that needs washing, and all the things a cowboy don't have to be perticular about, so long as they're out of the weather.

Unfolding a cowboy's bed and looking through it, a feller would find things in there that'd fit in with a parlor, bedroom, storeroom, and saddle shop. The kitchen is only a little ways off, by an open fire, and the living room takes in for as far as the eye can see, and away beyond that—all with the sky for a ceiling and the sun for heat and light.

Wherever the cowboy goes, his bed, or "thirty years' gathering," goes with him, even if he goes to town to stay for a spell and uses the hotel bed, his own roll will be in the corner of the room or

All with the sky for a ceiling and the sun for heat and light.

somewheres close, and only when going on a long trip, like to some rodeo where he might contest, does he leave his bed behind, because that bed, you might say, is his home. With it he's independent even if he's broke, and a cowboy sure does love to be independent.

The cowboy's bed, with all that's in it, weighs around from a hundred to a hundred and fifty pounds. It's a bed a feller can spread on the ground and sleep into and be comfortable, whether it's sixty below or above. At round-up time the bed is rolled and hauled around in the bed wagon from one camping place to another; and when the cowboy decides to drift by his lonesome and hit for new territories, he spreads the bed over a pack horse's back, the canvas tarp, being turned at both ends and snapped, keeps everything in there as it is; and when the end of the day comes and the squaw hitch is took off, the bed is slipped to the ground, ready to crawl into, and with hardly a wrinkle through the whole length of it.

I knowed riders who sported beds that cost as high as two hundred dollars. There'd be double blankets of fine Mexican weave which was light but would turn water and cold and heat, and all the rest tallying up till it seemed to me like real luxury—a "gathering" of the kind that'd be easier to get into than out of—but the pillow, wherever I went, was most generally always the same—it was always the war bag.

In the southern countries, on account of milder climate—which ain't so mild at times either—the beds are considerable lighter than they are up north. A lot of the cow foremen down there didn't allow a cowboy to have much bedding on account of the room and weight the wagons or pack outfits was scarce of when moving camp. Many of the outfits made the boys double up so as to save taking so much bedding, but down there, the same as up north, the bedroll was made up of pretty well of the same "gathering," and anything from a spur strap to a serge suit could be found among the soogans.

The true cowboy, whether he's at a cow camp, among his kind, or anywhere else, never wants to impose on anybody. Like any man who has a profession or trade, he has all that's necessary for him to follow up his line with, and you can always recognize him by that and the way he's got his outfit together.

Like, for instance, the true cowboy is always riding a good horse, the pick of many geldings, and never a shaggy cayuse. His riggin', even though wore, will be neat and strong, and the rider will be setting up on it straight, never slouchy, for a slouchy rider never has rode a bad horse.

And while drifting that way, the true cowboy, as I've said before, always has his bed along. While setting on one good horse he'll be leading another, and on that other will be his "thirty years' gathering" neatly packed and tied with a squaw hitch or double S.

There is, of course, exceptions, and I've seen good hands with a poor bed or none at all, but very seldom—as seldom as you'd see a good roper with a poor rope or a flapper with cotton socks.

I've heard old-timers tell of how they've slept in their saddle blankets more than in beds. I've slept lots of times without a bed, too, and so has every cowboy, but I can't say I'd refused a bed if it'd been around, and when I did cuddle up among the rocks and sagebrush without my bedroll, you can bet your boots it wasn't my fault. It was either that I'd stayed in town a few days too long or else I'd left my pack horse and bed behind so I could travel light and unhindered.

Like the old-timers, the reason they couldn't have much bedding with 'em was because they had to do a lot of light traveling. Indians would often make 'em leave their "thirty years' gathering" behind on account that leading a pack horse a feller couldn't travel so well, and speed meant life, or freedom, if it was a posse. Then again the old-time outfits didn't allow a cowboy many blankets on account they'd take too much room in the round-up wagon; and even though them old-timers liked to tell of how few beds they'd seen in their days, I don't reckon any of 'em would of refused one if it'd been handy, and I notice nowadays that it takes a mighty good pack horse to travel along under all they've gathered in soogans and blankets.

It's natural for a feller to get all the comforts there is, and the cowboy is as inclined to them comforts as anybody else, but when I see folks going camping nowadays, it strikes me like the cowboy took very little even if he'd went the limit. I never seen a cowboy use

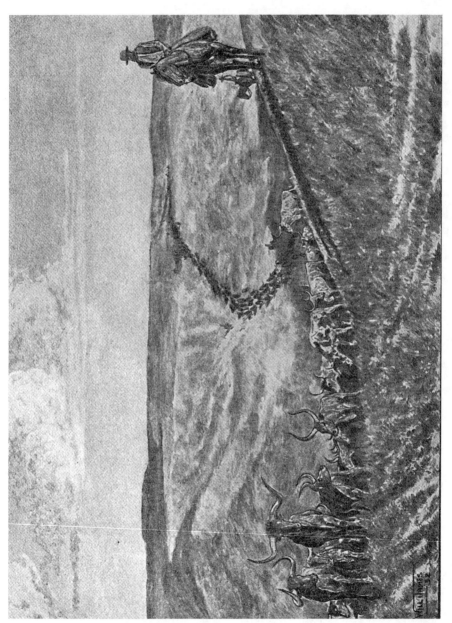

Like the old-timers, the reason they wouldn't have much bedding along was because they had to do a lot of light traveling.

a folding cot on the range—the ground is always plenty good—and the new-fangled sleeping bags and air mattresses and pillows are not being used by the riders. Them things might break or puncture. The cowboy's bed is still the same as it ever was; he still uses the soogans and blankets, and covers it all up with the same long canvas tarp.

With that "gathering" on a good pack horse he can drift along, and he never cares, when night comes, whether he finds a camp or ranch to put up at. He's free as the hawk above him, and when he strikes a cow or horse outfit that's worth his talents he's still free. It's the kind of work he's cut out for, he savvies, and nobody tells him what to do. He gets plenty of horses to ride, new country to see, and when he's ready to drift again, there's always his two private horses which's had a long rest and are just as hankering to hit for new territory as he might be.

So, wherever he's at, whether he's working or drifting, when the cowboy throws back the soogans of early morning he's at home. Among his "thirty years' gathering" with his two ponies close by and the sun coloring up the big country around, he's more than a king in a castle and kingdom, for he can go to sleep and wake up with no fear of ever being dethroned.

WHY THE HIGH HEELS?

Of all the details that's wondered at in the cowboy's clothes and rig, the high-heeled boots seem to hold a big share of the interest, and not knowing, some folks go as far as to make the mistake of thinking that the cowboy wears his neat-fitting, high-heeled boots for style and good looks.

Of course, any man, anywhere, whether he be hanging on a strap in a Subway train in New York or riding a bronc in a sagebrush flat in Arizona is entitled to some pride as to what he puts his feet inside of. The cowboy does take a powerful lot of pride in his boots, and even though his wages on the range might only be sixty dollars a month, he'll put out on an average of thirty dollars and more for a good pair of boots.

Them boots are handmade, and to order. The cowboy'll spread an order blank on the bunk-house floor of the cow camp, put his stocking foot on the paper, and with a pencil trace a line that marks the outside boundary of the territory that foot takes in. As a rule it averages pretty small, and I know many a hundred and eighty pound cowboy who could easy wear a size six shoe, or even a five.

The tape measure every boot maker sends out is another way of making sure of getting a snug fit. The measurement of the ball of the foot is marked down, then the low instep, the high instep, the heel, and then the calf, and last the height of boot top that's wanted, a few remarks are wrote down as to the fancy stitching on the boot tops, a little is said about the height of the heel, the style of the toe, and so on, and then the order is carefully folded into an envelope and lays at the camp till somebody comes by to take it to town and mail it.

Sometimes the letter don't get to town for two months, then another month is took up in the making of the boots, and after that the cowboy has to wait some more till somebody from the outfit goes in and brings the boots out to him. If the cowboy is lucky enough to have a horse fall on him and get a leg broke so he might go to town hisself, why then he might get the new boots before the old ones are wore out.

As a rule the cowboy orders his boots in winter and at least six months before he'll need 'em. The boots will wear him from one to two years, and sometimes even more. I had one pair of boots give me over two years of steady wear, and all I had done to 'em in that time was getting the heel built up again so I couldn't kick my foot through the stirrup.

So when you take it that a pair of boots last a man that long, it ain't no more than right that that man should be a little perticular as to how that boot looks. But the main thing that counts is how the boot feels when the man is in action.

In the everyday work of the cowboy there's happenings which call for action the likes of which would tally up well with that of the panther. That action starts from the point of the spike heels and backs the man that wears 'em to a sure footing and a holt wherever he lands.

Like, for instance, me and another feller was loping along on down the side of a mountain one time and hazing a pretty spooky bunch of ponies. My pardner was riding a bronc that'd just been caught out of the wild bunch a few days before, and that bronc wasn't at all what you'd call well mannered. We was a-hightailing it through the scrub pine and juniper, and doing pretty well in keeping track of the dust of the ponies we was following, when all at once I hear a crash which sounded like part of the mountain was giving way. My horse started to stampede, but I headed him for a low scrub pine and stopped him there; then I looked back, and mixed up in a patch of dead juniper trees I sees my pardner and his horse. That pony had gone on a rampage, and the way he was tearing things up it seemed like he had a grudge against dead junipers and everything in general.

But dry junipers ain't no soft thing to fool with, and with the little time I had to think I thought of the sharp hard limbs that would puncture that bronc and man right through, but luck seemed to be with 'em and the pony come out of an opening in the tangle all at once, and lit into a stampeding run down through the thick timber.

There was nothing I could do, I couldn't get my scared horse within forty feet of the runaway, head-fighting bronc my pardner was on, and all I done was to holler at him to fall off. His horse was headed for a low overhanging limb of a scrub pine, and I could already see what that limb would do to him if he stayed in the saddle.

Things went so fast that it was hard to follow, and it seemed like my pardner was about to be cut in two by the big limb when I get a glimpse of him leaving the saddle, then two spiked boot heels in midair, a cloud of dust, and all was still. When I rode to where the dust had been stirred I came first to my pardner, standing up, and looking at his hands. The hackamore rope he'd held on to when quitting his horse had slid and burned its way near through the gloves he was wearing. The bronc was the whole length of the rope away and flat to the ground where he'd been jerked off his feet.

But what would of interested them that wonders about the high heels on our boots would of been what the ground told where my pardner quit his horse. There was two deep gashes in the earth where that cowboy first landed when his pony was going downhill at the speed of a runaway train. Then about twenty feet from there down was two more gashes, these last was longer and deeper and showed where the cowboy got his second footing and played on his rope till it was time for him to set on it and upset his bronc to a hard lay.

It's second nature with the cowboy, regardless of where he's at, whether he's out alone or with others, to hang on to his horse and to depend on no one to help him. That comes from riding alone most of the time, and being that camp or water is often many long miles away, it's up to him to see that he's never left afoot, and what's more, that he does the work he sets out to do, and on any kind of a horse.

Things went so fast it was hard to follow.

The high-heeled boots is one of the things that help the cowboy to do whatever his work calls for; the tops of 'em protect his legs from the rubbing of the stirrup leather and steady his ankles against any jolts; the shank and narrow toe finds and fits the stirrup; the high heel keeps the foot from the danger of having the foot slip through the stirrup and hang, and that same heel will give the cowboy a sure and quick footing on any kind of ground, and soon as he needs it. There's a lot of times when he has to dodge a flying hoof in saddling or handling a horse and at such times he sure can't afford to slip.

The Round-up Wagon

When springtime comes to the range and the cold winds and snows give way to warm breezes and green grass, is when long wagons that's been stored away through the winter begin to be wheeled out from under the long sheds to be sort of looked over and fixed, wherever the fixing is needed.

There's months ahead when them wagons will be needed to haul grub, pots and pans, ropes, rolls of bedding, branding irons, cowboys' belongings, wood and water, and all that's needed to make a round-up camp. Them is the round-up wagons, and there's no heart ever flutters more than the cowboy's when the time comes for them same wagons to primp up and make ready to line out for the open range. The winters are always long at the scattering cow camps, and even with all the hard riding that's connected with them places, it's always sort of lonesome, and spring always seems awful slow to come.

It's never really spring with a cowboy till them wagons are pulled out from under the sheds, and till he sees the round-up cook, with a big pan of hot water and lots of soap, a-scouring away at the chuck box and all places where grub is to be loaded. It's then round-up time and spring has come sure enough.

When we speak of the Wagon in the cow country, it means a heap more than what the name hints to, and here I'm going to try and tell of what all it takes to make up what is called the Round-up Wagon on a good-size cow outfit.

It's only about six years or so ago since I held my last job on such a Wagon as I want to describe, and to tell the truth, that cow outfit didn't only run one of them spreads, but they run three. The outfit is still running strong and the same as it was then, and I want to say that regardless of what all's been wrote and said on the passing of the West and the cowboy there's still quite a few such outfits. Their range is not fenced in and the land is not farmed. They're still running cattle and paying wages to cowboys.

First in line with the Round-up Wagon comes the pilot. The pilot is one of the boys who knows the country well and rides ahead to pick out the best crossing at the creeks and rivers, so as the outfit that follows won't get in a jam. The outfit follows him wherever he goes acrost country, and seldom is a road, if one is found, ever followed.

A ways behind the pilot comes the chuck wagon, all covered with dried, smoked and salted victuals, sacks of beans and flour, and sometimes sugar. At the back of the wagon is a high box with sup-posed-to-be-dustproof partitions for all the utensils. That chuck box also holds lick—sirup—pieces of salt pork, and all the main things to sort of season the grub with; and then there's one or two drawers that holds a few old cinch buckles, spare buttons, a spur without a mate, and all sorts of things a feller might need sometime. As a rule, all them things should be in the jockey box that's on the side of the wagon, and where the axle grease and such is kept, but as them boxes usually get filled up too soon, another safe place has got to be found.

Close to the chuck box is a penned-in place where many pots, big Dutch ovens, the round-up-pan pot hooks and all rub sides; then ahead of that is the heavy stuff in sacks and barrels, and all wrapped in a big canvas is the staff of life, the carcass of a beef. The cook's private bed roll rides on top, and there's bows along the wagon so that in stormy weather the whole is covered with a big canvas and kept dry.

The cook is boss and driver of the chuck wagon, and he's got to be able to drive as well or better than he can cook before he can qualify to handle such horses as his four or six horse team usually are.

Following the chuck wagon comes the bed wagon. That wagon is loaded high with fifteen or twenty rolls of tarpaulin-covered blankets and soogans. It's the kind of bed rolls that gives the cowboy a sure chance to rest in all kinds of weather through the short time he has to rest in. In that same wagon is a couple of bales of whale line—lasso rope—which some outfits are good enough to furnish their riders with; then there's picket ropes for the night horses, and the rope cable which is used for the round-up corral for the saddle horses. At the bottom of that wagon can also be found a couple of sets of crutches for the boys that's layed up with a broken leg or ankle.

The flunkey drives that wagon, and as a rule that young feller's main trouble is of handling the ribbons—lines—of his four horse so that he can keep up with the cook and pilot without upsetting his wagon or having his team run away with him before the next camp ground is reached.

Close in the dust of the bed wagon comes the wood-and-water wagon. That extra wagon is used in prairie and desert countries where wood and water ain't as plentiful as it might be. That wagon is mostly to save time when it's necessary to make a dry camp; when a meal has to be got up in a hurry and some branding has to be done. The nighthawk—rider who herds the saddle horses at night—is the man who drives that wagon. As a rule he's too sleepy to care how fast the pilot leads out, and where to; all he cares about is to get to the next camp ground so he can have his sleep. If the pilot don't set too fast a gait, there's still some more to follow close—that's the remuda—the herd of saddle horses. The leader of them likes to follow the last wagon. There's on an average of two hundred saddle horses in a good-size remuda—about ten horses to the man—and furnished by the company.

All that which I've just described is what goes to make up the Wagon, and goes as one. It's sometimes called the Works, the Spread or the Layout, and makes camp where it's most handy for the riders while they're combing the country of cattle. The Wagon moves to a new camp ground most every day, and before sunup. The moves seldom take more than two hours from the time the old camp starts being tore down till the new camp is set up and the cook has his fire going again at the new camp ten or fifteen miles away. I used to know a cook who'd let his team run away near every time he moved camp, and, of course, the rest of the outfit followed—men and horses all enjoying it to the limit. Most round-up-wagon horses of such a outfit as I'm telling of here would be no good for anything else. They are spoiled to that job, fat and sassy all the time, and they are like relay horses in a racing team.

The Wagon is the cowboy's home while he's on round-up. Wherever it's camped is where the herds are brought to be worked—branding or cutting out. It's at the Wagon that he gets his fresh horses, his meals and his rest. And the Wagon is always at some place handy for that purpose. The Wagon is out and covering the range near all summer in some countries, and from calf-branding time till the

I used to know a cook who'd let his team run away near every time he moved camp.

In such places the camp is moved on pack mules.

beef is shipped in the fall. It always uses the same camp ground every year at the same time, and the work of each man, from the horse wrangler to the top hand and wagon boss, is like clockwork, and running on a system that would tally up with any smooth-running big business.

There's many other kinds of Wagons outside the one I've just tried to describe. In some countries, and even with big outfits, they crowd everything into one wagon. The cowboys are allowed only so much bedding, and no more, and other things are cut down according-ing. That's mostly in countries that's rough and when some kind of road has to be followed. Then there's range land to the south where wagons are plumb useless on account of it being so rough and brushy. In such places the camp is moved on pack horses or mules.

But whatever kind of Wagon it might be—whether it took three wagons or just one to make up the Layout, and whether it was all scattered on pack horses or mules—there's one thing I can never say against the Spread, and that is that it ever failed us. It never mattered whether it rained or hailed or snowed and the whole country was a bog, it was always there, and the cook was always by the fire a-tending to his pots when we came in to the new camp with a herd.

RANGE TABLE ETIQUETTE

The range table, if such it can be called, takes in quite a bit of territory. It spreads from the flap board of the chuck box, which is fastened at the hind end of the chuck wagon, to the pot rack at the fire and all around it. It's at them places that the victuals are gathered, and it's when the cowboys come a-loping into camp that the range table is complete, for it also takes in the cowboy's lap.

The flap board of the chuck box is the first place to hit for, for there is where the tin cups and plates are stacked, also knives and forks, and chili peppers and other seasonings. Then a circle around the fire is made and helpings are took out of the skillets and dutch ovens which are in the ground and surrounded with hot ashes. There's beef, potatoes, biscuits, and coffee, three times a day, and nobody hankers for a change much, unless it'd be for some of the ham and eggs that'd been tasted in town, quite some time back.

But ham and eggs or any other fancy dish wouldn't take the place of beef for long with a cowboy, and even though he's gut-shrunk and a light eater he likes things that are plain and which'll fill him up the quickest, for, to prove himself a hand, he don't spare much time to eat, and it's all to his credit if he's the first one through and ready to go on a fresh-caught horse.

Fifteen minutes from the time he rides in he ought to be ready to ride out again. In them fifteen minutes he unsaddles his tired horse and turns him loose, grabs a plate and eats, and then ropes another horse and has him ready to top off. Of course there's no set time as to how long the meal and change of horses should take, but fifteen minutes would about make it, often less than that, and the rider who is always last in being ready is never thought much of as a cowboy.

I remember, when I was still much of a kid and was promoted from horse wrangling to riding with the boys, I'd got an awful fear of being the last one to be through eating and have my horse caught and saddled. I hadn't stopped shooting up in length as yet and had some pretty fair appetite, and many a time, so I wouldn't be last, I'd rush over to the corral, rope a fresh horse and saddle him, with a biscuit still in my mouth.

But as I went on riding for different outfits year after year, I'd got so my appetite sort of gauged itself—it got to looking forward to one good meal a day, and that was in the evening. The evening meal is the best because the work is all through for a spell then, all excepting for them who are on "cocktail" shift, and the riders can take all the time they want without taking the risk of being disgraced for being the last one out.

I've seen some meals put away in mighty quick time, specially when there's two circles made a day, and herds to be worked between times. It seemed like we'd no more than reach camp when we'd be riding out again, but as little a time as it takes a cowboy to eat I never hardly seen any of 'em bolt their food down. They just eat less. Then again, being the cowboy never gathers around the chuck wagon to hold meetings or discuss social problems, and how he can go right ahead and help himself instead of waiting for orders or courses, all goes to making a quick job of a meal.

But, as hurried as the morning and noon meals are, nobody really seems to hurry, it's just like as if them meals are over with

Fifteen minutes from the time he rides in he ought to be able to ride out again.

quick, and that's about all. There's no rushing of the chuck box and ovens, and no rider does any crowding of the others, nor over-reaching. That all would be a mighty untolerated breach of etiquette, for there is etiquette a-plenty at the range table, even if there is no table, and even if all hands do keep their hats, and chaps, and spurs on while they eat.

It's etiquette that's fitting of the range and with as high a standard as any that's ever showed under the cut glass chandeliers. The cowboy eats because he's hungry, and if he does eat with his knife once in a while he does it because the knife might be more fitted than the fork, but he don't do it nowheres like he's pictured to, and many of 'em use their utensils according to Hoyle.

But that doesn't matter so much anyway, there's other things more important, and which is all mighty good manners. Like for instance, when a cowboy lifts a dutch-oven lid for a helping, he makes sure not to lay the lid where the under part will touch sand, and be careful not to stir up dust while the oven is open. If the wind is blowing he'll skirt around the other riders and on the right side so none of the dust he might stir would fly in their plates. If he pulls a skillet off the coals, he'll put it back after he's through so it'll be hot for the others also.

When a rider gets up for a second cup of coffee and while he's helping hisself another rider hollers "man at the pot" the rider up has to pass the coffee around to all of them that want it before he sits down again. Every man considers the other through every meal and will do all he can to be as much of a hand at that as he does at roping or riding.

I remember an old cowman one time who'd joined the round-up wagon for a few days. Some of his cattle had strayed in that country and he'd come along to gather 'em and take 'em back. He'd brought his kid with him, about fifteen he was, and a pretty good hand too for his age, but he'd never been away from the home range much, and he seemed to develop an awful appetite soon as he struck the wagon. It was a change of grub for him.

He took on a real man-sized feed one evening and his dad was sort of watching with a surprised and pleased look. All went well till come time for the kid to get up for a second helping of boiled rice and raisins, and when he started to help himself the second time his dad was there alongside of him. The kid looked up at him, and, understanding the look in his face, he dropped the spoon like it was a hot iron. All the old cowman said was, "There's others, son."

But that was a-plenty and the kid would rather took a beating than be caught playing pig in front of all the riders, only his growing appetite had got the best of him and he'd forgot himself.

That's a small example of a young cowboy's training at range table etiquette. There's no set rules to that training and nothing much is ever said about it. It all originates natural-like from a life in the open and through the principle of the men that follows it.

If a man is a good cowboy and takes pride in being a hand he'll also take pride in doing the right thing around the chuck wagon, he'll consider the others and not do anything that would go against the unmapped rules of range table etiquette.

After he's through eating he'll see that whatever is left on his plate is thrown far from the camp and to the chipmunks and birds, that his cup is emptied, all utensils picked up and all put in "the round-up pan" which the cook sets by the chuck wagon for that purpose.

The way the cowboy sets himself down to eat might be some more etiquette. He never spraddles all over the ground; instead he crosses both feet, while balancing a plate in one hand and a cup in the other, and bends his knees, and comes down to rest on the flat of his spurred boots. The plate is never layed on the ground, it lays

45

He never spraddles all over the ground.

between his knees, and only the cup touches the sod, by one knee and within easy reach.

When he gets up he springs up, never using a hand to help himself with, for in one hand he has the plate and in the other the cup.

Even the old stove-up cowboys who can hardly bend a leg any more manage to follow up on range table etiquette that way, and I wonder sometimes if there ain't as much to live up to in that etiquette, if you want to be called "a hand," as there is around the linen-covered tables, if you want to be called "finished."

ON CIRCLE

Speaking of being on circle reminds me of one perticular outfit up here in Montana. The foreman of that outfit had the greatest way of leading out on that ride which we call circle than most any cow boss I ever seen, and that's where the reminding comes in at.

But before I go on to tell how that foreman used to lead out, I'd like to say that riding on circle don't mean that it's done in a circle. An outline of such a ride would most always take the shape of a jagged-edge triangle, one point of the triangle at the camp, for that's where the ride starts from and winds up at.

Now getting back to the cow foreman and his style, and to begin with, that feller was a mighty fast man at catching his horse and have him saddled up, and being it's against a cowboy's religion to be a drag at anything, we sure all tried to keep up with him; but he had the best of us; his horses was most all what we called gentle, and he had a considerable easier time saddling up than most any of us did.

On circle is when we'd ride stout broncs or horses that was too ornery to take interest in working a herd; they would be the kind that was only good to chase a critter with, and it sure took a cowboy to make 'em do that.

With them kind of ponies to rope and drag out and saddle, it was no wonder that the foreman was near always the first man to have his horse saddled and ready to go, but that didn't keep none of us from trying to be close second. It sure was always a contest and where the steady loser would be considered a poor hand and a drag.

WILL JAMES
'30

On circle is when we'd ride stout broncs or horses that was too ornery to take interest in working a herd.

47

The first saddling of the day would be done by the light of the stars—and only a faint streak to the east showed that a new day was coming, sure enough. It was at the time of the day—or maybe I should say night—when the air is crimpy and ponies are full of snorts and aching for something to happen so they can warm up.

A-setting on his horse, the foreman would wait till all the boys had saddled and was mounted. He'd always act kinda restless, but soon enough the last man would be earing down his horse and easing hisself up on him; then the foreman, with a grin on his face, would take off his hat and even though there would be no sun as yet to shade his eyes from, he'd hold it in front of him, over his eyes and the direction we'd be riding circle that day. About that time he'd lean ahead close to his horse's ears and start that pony of his from a standstill to a high lope.

It was about then that things would happen around the round-up camp. The riders, none of 'em wanting to be drags, would start their ponies to follow up the foreman's lead, and them ponies' natural instincts would never let that chance to bust loose go by 'em. There'd be bellers from half of 'em and an awful strain on the cinches and latigos as they'd swell up into doing what was to their heart's content. Some would buck in a circle, others would line out in long hard-hitting jumps any old direction, and a few would stampede and leave the flats.

They all graded from hard buckers to stampeders and then crowhoppers. Some would just cut up a little, and the older ponies, like the older cowboys that was on 'em, would have a hankering to tear around some, but they wouldn't, much, and I always figgered they must of suffered some, because the spirit was still there. The older rider on top of 'em was the party that was responsible for the behaving. They wasn't caring to be shook up no more, and so, instead of busting out in a high lope from the jump, they'd ease their ponies into that gait gradual-like. That was all right for the older man, but when a young feller was seen pulling that kind of a stunt it didn't go so well.

If the foreman had wanted to, he could of lined out on circle without hardly any commotion—only maybe three or four of the ponies would of acted up any to speak of, but as that perticular feller would say: "If a horse is going to fight, I'd rather see him do it close to camp and not when a rider is out all by hisself." I didn't worry much about what he meant then, but now it comes to me that there was a lot of sound judgment in that. The foreman believed that when there's an ornery streak in a horse it should come out first thing, then better work could be expected. He was sure right and it worked well, because very few of the ponies would ever unlimber to buck again after the wild start from camp, for if anything was on their chest and aching to come out it'd sure come out then.

The foreman would keep on a high lope through the whole commotion. Once in a while he'd look back to see how everybody was a-setting, but that was very seldom. Pretty soon, and half a mile or so from camp, the riders, after getting their horses to behaving, would begin to catch up with him and keep in gait. The ponies'd had their fun, and breathing good, blood circulating in fine shape, horses and men lined out for the circle.

There is not many cow foremen that I know of who lead out on circle the way this one I just told about. I've rode with others who start from camp on a fast walk and dogtrot. I've rode for outfits that seldom broke into a lope till it come time to head off something. Every scope of country has a different way of working, but when it comes to riding circle it's all done pretty well the same, whether the start is slow or fast.

The ride which we call a circle starts from wherever the round-up wagon is camped, or from permanent cow camps the outfit has scattered over the range. The riders, counting from four to forty of 'em—depends on the size of the outfit—ride out together to a point away in the distance where they're to scatter from. In the countries to the north where water is a plenty, cattle are scattered everywheres, and there a knoll ten or twelve miles from camp is always picked to ride up on before the foreman does the scattering of his riders. He'll send his men by twos both ways till certain landmarks are reached where from there they're to head back for camp bringing in all the stock they find on the way.

It's up to the foreman to see that every man is paired off right, like, for instance, if a man is riding a special ornery horse he'll send another man with him on a good horse to do what the first man might not be able to on account of that horse. Another thing is the considering of strange riders who don't know that perticular country. With each one of them he's got to send one who does. Then there's the men who are riding young unbroke horses; he'll pair them off with others who are riding well-broke old ponies, and so on, till the last man high-tails it for his territory.

In the circle ride there's what we call the outside circle, which is the biggest ride and picked for the strongest and orneriest horses; then on down the line to the inside circle, which is the shortest ride and picked for the young horses. The circles between are all divided up according to the rider and what he might be riding. As for the foreman, he might be anywheres at any time.

Scattered the way they are, the riders form a long line combing the country of all stock toward camp. Long streaks of dust begin to appear as cattle are stirred from shade and stream. One rider finds one bunch, turns it over a ridge for another rider to keep moving, and then rides after another bunch. It all goes on that way till finally many little bunches form a few big ones. The line of riders gradually narrows and runs to a point, and when camp is reached

One rider finds one bunch, turns it over a ridge for another rider to keep moving and then rides after another bunch.

all the cattle found in that circle are run into one big herd, ready to work soon as fresh horses are caught.

In some countries two fast circles are made a day and fresh horses are caught for each ride. In other countries only one circle is made. It is slower and one horse has to do a man the whole day. I always liked the two-circle country best, because I always like fresh horses.

The Remuda

I was setting by the rope corral of the round-up camp one morning and watching the *remuda*—saddle-horse bunch—come in. There'd never been much chance of seeing it come in at sunup, on account that most always it would still be dark, with only a faint hint of daybreak, when the night-hawk—night herder—would have 'em all corralled and ready for us.

But that particular morning, as I sat there a-watching, there was sunlight over the range—early morning sunlight—and the reason of his being late—as the nighthawk told the foreman afterward—was that the heavy thundershowers through the night had spooked up the ponies pretty bad. They'd scattered and he'd lost a few of 'em; finding 'em again had took time.

That didn't go very well with the cow foreman. There's no room for excuses on the range, no matter how good they might be; but far as I was concerned the nighthawk could bring the *remuda* at sunup every morning—not that I minded saddling up at daybreak, but I liked the sight of them ponies coming in, with the low sun a-shining on 'em.

There was more than two hundred head of horses in that *remuda*, most all solid colors—a few with stocking legs and bald faces, no pintos. With the rich light of the early morning sun a-shining on the silky hides of them, it all made a mighty fine picture right there; but there was more to add on—a heap more. The shadows of the ponies run up against the foot of a long high ridge.

The top of that ridge was capped with white sandstone, which gradually turned to pink farther down, and then at the center of the ridge and running all along it the sandstone was red—a deep red. To tally up with all of that, the light green of the new spring grass run up the side of that ridge and plumb against that red rim; then, splitting the ridge in two, seemed like, was the high-soaring cloud of dust stirred by the *remuda*'s many hoofs, and looked like a veil a-hanging from the sky.

The *remuda* came on past the point of the ridge, and then the nighthawk turned 'em straight toward the corral. The picture it made faded away by thoughts of the work that was ahead for that day. Every cowboy was on the job with loop ready to catch their horses soon as they was corralled, and I hightailed it to my saddle to get my own rope.

With every good-sized, well-run outfit there is such a *remuda* as I've just told of. Each rider is furnished on the average of ten horses. At that rate twenty riders make up a bunch of two hundred saddle horses—that's what goes to make up the *remuda*. The *remuda* is always right on the tail of the round-up wagon, so that whenever the cowboys come in to eat they also can get a fresh horse. I used to wonder which I'd miss the most between a square meal and a fresh horse, and I've proved it to myself a few times since. I've always took the fresh horse.

Each ten head of horses the company furnishes the cowboy with is what you might call divided into four classes: Five or six of these ten go to make what we call "circle horses." These are used to round up cattle with. Two or three others are the day herd, or cutting horses. These are the top cow horses, used either in holding a herd, loose or close, or in cutting out stock from a herd and roping. Then there's one or two more that's called the night horses, which do the work around the bedded herd on night guard. Added onto these three classes of ponies there comes two or three broncs—unbroke horses. These uneddicated ponies fit in on small circles or in holding a herd, and it's all to how they're willing to learn and grab holt whether they're going to be just circle horses or valuable cow horses.

These different classes of horses goes to make one cowboy's string. Each horse has a job he's fitted for, and with the amount of them that's to every man, a horse is rode only a few hours in every two or three days. All the horses has to do the rest of the time is eat and sleep and follow the round-up wagon till their turn comes to be rode again. The cowboy changes horses three or four times a day.

There's many kinds of horses in a *remuda*. As many kinds as the count of 'em. I've never seen no two alike, nor two of which could be handled alike. One'll kick at you and go to bucking if you twist his ear to get on him, and another'll do that very same thing if you don't twist that ear of his. One has to be handled carelesslike or he'll tear things to pieces, and if you do that with another, things will be tore to pieces again.

But the bunch of ponies that draws the most interest in any *remuda* is what we call "the rough string"—and rough is a mighty tame name for them. In as big a bunch of horses as it takes to make a *remuda*, there's always bound to be a few whose natural feelings are all against man, saddle and work. Their only hankerings is to fight all of that, and being it's against the grain of the cowman to leave a perfect-built horse grow useless while some good horse does the work, he hires a bronc-fighting cowboy to get the work out of them ornery ponies. The work that's got out of 'em is mixed with a lot of fighting, and the result would often be of rough-string riders riding the bed wagon while recuperating from broken ribs and legs. In the

And rough is a mighty tame name for them.

meantime the ornery ponies would pile on more fat and then another cowboy would take 'em on.

The next to draw interest and also admiration from all hands is the good cow horse. He does his work and comes to the top after the bad horse has been bested and made to behave. There's quite a good sprinkling of them in every *remuda*, too, and with the other fair-to-middling and good horses that's gathered there, the *remuda* is not at all a bad place to throw a rope into, if you know what you're doing.

In some territories where the *remuda* is called "cavvy," they often use mares to lead and sort of hold the cavvy together with. The mare is belled, and with a colt usually following her it all kinda forms an attraction and keeps the gelding in one bunch; sometimes fighting one another for the privilege of being near the colt. That's as far up as I ever remember a mare getting on the range as a saddle animal. I don't remember ever seeing a cowboy riding a mare, or a cow outfit having a mare in a cavvy, unless she was a bell mare, and in countries where the saddle-horse bunch is called *remuda*—remooda—not even a bell mare is allowed. Old saddle horses that's not apt to try to stray away pack the bells, and the bells are for the nighthawk to count when the night is too dark to see.

They are also mighty useful during stormy nights when horses hunt for shelter—a gelding might graze away and lose the whereabouts of the *remuda* if it wasn't for the sound of the bells. Then again, there's something about 'em that draws a horse once he's used to hearing it; he'll follow the sound most anywhere and seldom ever stray away from it.

In parts of the cow country the remuda is herded night and day; the nighthawk herds 'em at night and the wrangler tends to 'em during the day.

The wrangler also hazes 'em as the round-up wagon moves to a new camp, and corrals 'em whenever it's time for the cowboys to change horses.

In some of the desert and mesa countries and where the wrangler is called "cavvy wrango" they seldom ever night-herd. The cavvy wrango shoves the ponies up a mesa where the getting down is hard, and goes and gets 'em in the morning while the cook is wrastling the pots. In the brush and rocky countries of the South they hobble most of the horses for the night—it would be a hard country to night-herd in anyway.

But whatever the difference might be with the *remuda* from one country to another, there hasn't been no change, and there'll never be no change as long as there's range left. There'll be range for many, many years yet, and regardless of all the inventions that's took the horse away from his work, there's nothing will ever be invented that'll ever take the place of the ponies that go to make up the *remuda*.

WILL JAMES
'30

There's nothing will ever be invented that'll ever take the place of the ponies that go to make up the remuda.

HOOKS

Of all that's necessary in the cowboy's outfit, his hooks, or spurs, are amongst that, and not far from being what he needs the most. They're not on his heels as an ornament, even though some of them steels might be decorated a whole lot, and they sure take a big share of the credit for the way the work is done on the range.

The big share for that credit is in the way they're handled, and the cowboy is the feller that knows how to handle 'em. He's raised with them on his heels, and by the time he's half grown they're as much part of him as his two hands, and near as useful, for it's with them that the hand and eye work.

Like with the throw of a rope, for instance, most good rope horses are apt to check up too soon when they see the whale line sail towards a critter's horns, they want to brace themselves for a jerk, and stopping too soon that way has spoiled many a good catch by an inch. That's on account of some horses not heeding the spur, but as a rule a little touch of it at such a time always does the work, and there's no checking up till the loop is drawed around both horns.

Even the wisest and freest of horses need the spur as a reminder that way once in a while; they know their work so well that they're apt to get careless, specially when a little tired, and it's up to the cowboy to remind 'em of what's to be done; it's him who knows that one step short in roping or cutting out will mean more work.

Then again, even with the most willing horse, there's many places in the range country that he don't care to drop into or go over the top of, and it takes a little persuading from the spur to get him to go on. If the cowboy was riding for pleasure he might go around such places, but there's work to be done when he rides, and often a short cut acrost rough country is mighty necessary to head off a bunch that's needed.

But with the good willing horse, it's seldom that the spur ever touches his hide. The cowboy, knowing how to handle the steel, threatens with 'em a heap more than he touches, and a motion of the leg is about all such a horse ever feels. But even with the horse that needs the spur, there's no gouging or cutting done. That's against cowboy principle, and any man that's caught using too much spur on a horse is not thought much of around any cow camp. Things'll most likely get so hot for him around there that he'll soon think of other places.

I know of a few such instances, one where some overgrown would-be cowboy cut a little gash in a gentle horse's side one time. The wagon boss had hired him because he was short-handed, but when he seen the spur mark on the horse he figgered he'd a heap rather get along without him, but he teached him a lesson first; he gave him a brand-new string of ponies, all rough ones, and after he got through pointing 'em out to him, he says:

He'd rather hear 'em jingle
than to jab with 'em.

"Now, young feller, let's see you put spur marks on them horses."

The "young feller" didn't get to put no spur marks on them horses; he was too busy finding something to hang onto, and the few he tried to ride left their marks on him instead. The next morning he caught his own horse, asked for the few days' wages he had coming, and hit out, and I think he was careful never to cut a gentle horse after that. Fact is, I know he was, because it wasn't over three months later when I seen him driving a storage-house truck in town.

I never seen a real cowboy cut a horse with his spurs. If he ever does, it's sure by accident, and the horse wouldn't feel half as hurt about it as he would. Even with the bad horse—the kind that needs lots of persuading to straighten up and get any work out of—the spur is brought to work mostly as a nerve tickler, like the tip of the finger against any live human's ribs, and the steel is never used as a cutting machine, for there wouldn't be no advantage to that.

Just the other day the Antler round-up wagon camped on the creek to within a couple of miles of my corrals. My "spread" is in the heart of the Antler range, and when the outfit comes close that way I always throw in with 'em for the day or two to sort of unlimber my rope arm. They had a remuda of a hundred and thirty head; them horses had been rode hard since early spring, and even though I never looked for such signs, I'll bet there wasn't a spur mark on any one of them. I know that without looking, because, at one time, I've worked for many such outfits, and I know that a spur mark don't go well there.

The true cowboy takes great pride in being good to a horse, and if the spurs was unnecessary and cruel he'd never wear 'em. They can be used cruelly, of course, but any man that knows how to use them and what their purpose is will never be cruel with 'em. It's usually the feller that's rode but little who does the damage with the spurs.

When the cowboy buys a pair of spurs, the first thing he generally does is go to work on the rowels with a file. He'll file all the sharp edges off every point of them rowels and till all are smooth and dull; but to the folks who don't know spurs and how they're used, the long points of a two-inch rowel still looks mighty wicked. I know, for a fact, of many persons who thought that whenever a cowboy hit a horse with the spur the rowel was sunk in the flesh plum to the shank. According to that, it was no wonder to me why they thought our spurs was cruel. There's many who thinks that the bigger rowel a spur has the more cruel it is. That's again from the idea that the whole rowel is sunk in every time. If that was done a horse would keel over at the first sinking.

The bigger and thicker the rowel is and the more points there is to it, the less harm it'll do. It's the small thin rowel with the few points that does the damage. A rowel of few points lets loose hide wrinkle in between, and that gives a chance for the points to cut, more so with the small rowel, because there's not so much play as there is with the big one; they won't turn so easy, and a jab with 'em is more steady and solid. Any rider could take a five-point, three-quarter rowel and cut a horse to pieces, if he had a mind to, where with a two-inch "sunset" rowel, which has many points close together, he could just ruffle the hair and no more. The old-time nickel-plated army spur, with the small sharp rowel about the size of a dime, was the most cruel spur I ever seen. I'm glad to see that now'days the army spur has no rowel at all, and whoever is responsible for that ought to have a medal as big as the Statue of Liberty, all incrusted with diamonds.

I'm talking of spurs at their worst now; but like anything else, if handled right, they sure have their qualities, too, and they're mighty necessary—so necessary that out here on the range the cowboy never takes 'em off his boots. For with him changing horses from two to

He ain't apt to wonder if he'll need his spurs on this or that horse. That's all settled by keeping them spurs on always.

four times a day during the round-ups, riding many that are strange at other times and with all kinds of dispositions, he ain't apt to wonder if he'll need his spurs on this or that horse. That's all settled by keeping them spurs on always—always, excepting when he goes to town or to some far-off shindig, and as usual the spur never comes off the boot till that boot is wore out; then it goes on to stay on another pair till it's wore out, and so on. At night them boots are pulled off with the help of the spurs, like with a bootjack, and when the boots are slipped on of early morning the spur is part of 'em.

Whatever the cowboy does—wrassling calves, branding, roping or riding—whether he's afoot or on horseback, the spurs are always jingling at his heels. He'll never stumble over 'em; they been there too long. And they come into his work as natural-like as the crook that comes into his elbow while he's eating.

He uses 'em unthinking, whether he's riding a bad horse or a good one. On the bad horse them spurs will act as a sort of feeler as to where the horse might be at every jump, sometimes reaching for a holt when the sitting is uncertain, and then, by the tattoo that's played with 'em, the horse will soon be convinced that this tearing things up ain't getting him nothing but an uncomfortable feeling from both sides. But the hide will seldom be marred by any scratches, for the cowboy knows his spurs; he knows that a little jab with 'em will do all he wants 'em to.

While riding a gentle horse and all is going well, them spurs will just set there on the cowboy's heels and jingle. They're music to his ears always, the heartbeats of the life he's living; he'd rather hear 'em jingle than to jab with 'em, for while they're just jingling everything is okay and in harmony.

III

THE CRITTER

When we say "critter" out here on the range we mean cow, the word "cow" stands for cattle in general. We'd speak of some feller "punching cows" for an outfit while that same feller might be handling nothing but steers, and the whole bovine family, wether they're papas or mamas, sons or granddaughters, all are called cows by the range rider, or critters. Of course that's speaking of 'em in a general way. It's different when a certain animal is pointed out, then it's classed as a he or she, as "that two-year-old steer" or "that brockle-faced heifer," outside of sorting out stuff that way, they all file in under the name of cows or critters.

Critter is short for crethure, and I'm told that crethure stands for most anything that breathes. Maybe that's why I've heard some old cowboys put the name of critter on other animals besides the cow, of course that was very seldom and in mighty few parts of the range country, for, as a rule critter belongs to the cow only.

Like the other day, I was riding with the cow foreman of a neighboring outfit, and him and me got to arguing as to what that speck was on a high ridge about three miles from us all by itself. Finally I bet him a dollar that that speck was a critter, he called me and said that it was a horse. When we got closer we seen that it was a horse, but if a critter, or crethure, stands for most anything that breathes, why I'd won too. Anyway, I still owe him that dollar.

The critter (I'll keep on calling range cattle by that) is the mean-eyed, sharp-horned, kink-tailed animal that cowboys or any others

She'll hit for the brush at round-up time and chase the cowboy
back on his horse if he tries to get in there to get her out.

that know her don't fall in love with. She's ungrateful, independent and ornery, that's because she's pretty wild and can rustle a living without the help of man, that is, in most countries, but, wether she gets help or not, she sure don't never show any appreciation. Just let the green grass come and see what happens. There won't be no mild nor thankful look in her eye for the hay that was handed her when the drifts was deep, and she won't beller no thanks for being pulled out of the bog she'd got into, instead she'll hit for the brush at round-up time and chase the cowboy back on his horse if he tries to get in there to get her out.

But even at that there's many good points about her, (by her, I'm taking the critter in general, the whole family, and all he's and she's of range stuff). For one thing, she brings a considerable on the hoof, she decorates our table with the staff of life, beef. Then again, her hide makes fine saddles, and shoes, and suit cases. Of course you can't figger on her milk because her little "Johnny" calf gets that, and besides she ain't the milking kind anyhow, her spirit won't allow her calf to be robbed, and that's some more to the credit of the Critter. All cow outfits buy milk in the can, that is if they are a mind to, if not, the coffee is drunk black, and that goes well.

I remember one of the times when I had to drink my coffee black, all on account of a little calf too. I'd rode up onto him while I was riding line one day and found this little feller, about a day old, alongside his dead mammy and butting her to get up. I caught the calf, and after blindfolding my horse, got him into the saddle. The ride into camp was kind of rough for the both of us but I finally got him there and begin pouring diluded canned milk down his throat. He got so he begin to drink it out of a bucket, and after ten days I run out of canned milk. From then on I'd run in a bunch of she stuff, dab my rope on the biggest, milk 'em while they was down, and that way get enough milk to keep little Johnny alive. That was

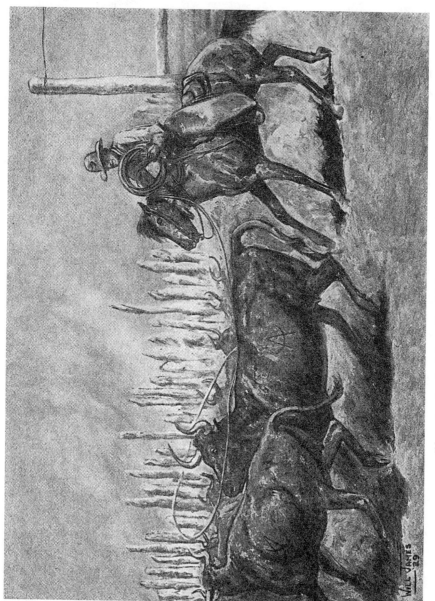

I'd run in a bunch of she stuff and dab my rope on the biggest.

the first and last time I'd ever milked a cow, but the calf lived. I know that for a fact, because it wasn't over a year later when he tried to hook my horse just because I wouldn't let him quit the herd.

That's another thing about the critter, they're fighting fools, of course they fight at the wrong time sometimes, like that calf did, and that's what keeps a cowboy from having any sentiments for 'em, but them same fighting qualities is often what keeps 'em going, they'll fight the blizzards and droughts the same way, and if they get down they fight some more and till the last breath goes out of 'em. The result is, not many get down, and the wolf keeps a hunting for rabbits.

But the greatest spirit shows up in the critter when the scared bellers of a young calf is heard. The mammy don't take long in answering that call, and besides, there's many sharp-horned steers right alongside of her to see what there is around they can tear up. Any enemy goes then, wether it's a wolf, bear, or cougar.

The steers, not having any responsibilities, only to get fat, are always great protectors in a herd. I've seen it in the southern countries, where the water is scarce, of some lone steer watch over the calves that was hid while their mammies went to water. (The mother always hides a young calf before going to water, which is sometimes ten miles away.) He'd maybe have three or four to take care of and none of the calves would get out of his sight, for, as young as them little fellers was, their instinct, which is the critter's, told 'em they was safe to get out of their hiding place and stretch while the big feller was around.

If the big feller ain't around the little calf knows better than to even wiggle an ear while his mammy is gone. He'll flatten down in the hiding place he was left at and play possum wether he wants to or not. His instinct tells him to be still. No wolf would ever find him, because, as some old timers claim, and I sure believe it myself, a young calf don't throw no scent, breeze or no breeze.

But a calf, like any other young one, begin to get smart after a certain age, too smart, and at a few weeks old they don't care to hide much no more. They either follow their mammies on the long trip to water or else hide a little while till she's gone, then buck and play around, and hide some more just before she gets back. When they hear her come back they're plum innocent and just beller their hunger.

When they get that smart, a wolf can seldom get 'em any more, for, by that time, they can run plenty fast so they can reach the protection of another herd before the wolf gets a holt with his fangs. As far as the cayote is concerned, he's left away in the background, they're too wiry for him by then.

Another good point about the critter is that she never forgets as to where she left her calf last, the same with the calf, no matter how young, he never forgets where he seen his mammy last either. In case either of 'em stray off, when the calf gets hungry and the cow's bag fills up, they sure both know where to meet again, and that's only from a few hundred yards from where they last seen one another. If one is missing the other will wait and beller, the same as to say "I'm here, where are you?"

I've went along on many a long drive with herds of mixed stuff. The little calves most always hung along behind the drive and amongst the "drags" (weak stuff), their mammies would sometimes be away off in the lead a mile or so ahead. All was fine and dandy till along about the time the herd was bunched up when some of them little calves would get to realizing they was hungry and remembering where they seen their mammies last, that was about ten miles back. In the confusion of the big herd, hearing lots of bellers and none they recognized, them little fellers would break past a rider and start hightailing it back to where they come. Their speed, even tho they was young and had traveled a long stretch of hot and dusty trail, was near like that of an antelope for a few miles, and it took a mighty good horse to catch up with 'em, many a time they couldn't be turned when they was caught up with and then the riders would just have to rope the little fellers and lead 'em back or else pack 'em.

There'd be no peace till the calves found their mammies in that herd, and then, the next morning when the herd moved on again for another day's drive, there'd be another separation for the day, the cows in the lead and the calves amongst the drags, more hard riding at the end of the day and finally the peaceful reunion.

To folks who've seen and handled only the gentle tempered dairy stock the wild eyed range critter would most likely be mighty strange and draw no interest much. For one thing the range cow is not very heavy on the milk supply, she just manages to have enough for a fine big calf and would lower her horns at any human who would try to cheat that calf. They're not raised for milk anyway only for beef. That reminds me of an old story that's been running out here ever since I can remember. There was some high-up foreigner came West one time and asked an old cowman how many cattle he owned. "Well," says the old cowman, "I paid taxes on twenty thousand head last year." —"Impossible," says the stranger. "Why, where would you get all the milk maids to milk all them cows?"

The range critter don't know what bran-mash and a stable is, she's lucky if, in the northern states, she has a willow shed to go into while the blizzard is howling. In that same country she is, nowdays, fed some wild hay and the critter comes to it the same as an elk does, only to keep going till the snow goes and grass comes. All her tallow is from the same kind of grass or brush that was in the country many centuries ago.

With that and her natural wild instinct, even tho she's bred up a considerable nowdays, the range critter, with all her ornery ways, is due to a lot of respect, she'll fight and rustle for herself and her kind, she's plum against milking machines and having her little calf be cheated out of milk and being stunted, and besides that, no matter what us fellers call her at times, she sure does bring beef.

IV
ALL IN THE DAY'S RIDING

BLIND BUCKERS

I guess most everybody nowadays has seen a bucking horse, there's plenty of them in all the good rodeos that's being pulled off all over U.S.A. every year starting from July and lasting till the following February. They're bucking horses natural, inclined that way just the same as any human might be inclined to be bad, and the people that's missed seeing them have missed a whole lot worth seeing. Them horses are the picked bad ones from the big ranges of our western country, and the riders who follow 'em from here to wherever the horses are shipped *sure* have to be good ones, if they're going to win any money riding 'em.

With the folks that's seen horses buck acrost the arena at the rodeos the few instances I'm going to tell of now will be easy to understand, all that has to be done will be to know that the horse is not in an arena, no tall fence to turn him and no rider to haze the horse where he belongs. I'm going to tell of blind buckers, wild horses that don't care where they hit nor how, while a rider is on 'em.

Such horses are apt to show that meanness any place of course, and there's been many of 'em go thru the solid fences of the arenas. I had a horse go thru a four foot woven wire fence out of an arena with me one time, he bucked halfways up the bleachers, scattered the crowd, splintered the timbers and bucked all the way back down into the arena without even stumbling. I seen another horse try that

73

another time and he was left hung on one of the big splintered timbers.

Them is what I call blind buckers. When they're loose and no rider is on 'em you couldn't pull 'em towards a crowd with a steam engine, but the minute a rider climbs 'em they don't care where they go, they're blind mad. They're willing to commit suicide so as they can commit murder.

I seen a horse buck out of an arena once, knock two men down, dive into an automobile and buck over the top of it. I'd brought that same horse to town with a bunch a while before and, as an automobile come along the road, he quit the bunch like a scared rabbit, went thru a fence and hightailed it acrost a field. I sure had to ride some to get him back.

It's hard for folks that's used to the gentle barn-raised horse to know the actions of our horses. The western range horse is just as different to the eastern gentle-raised horse as a lynx is to the purring kitten by the stove. Even when tamed down the western range horse has tricks that are entirely different from the eastern horse. I'm now talking of horses that's rode on the range, not them that's rented out to tourists.

I was breaking horses on contract with a feller one time. The country was scary to break horses in. It was rough, high mountains and timber everywhere, and right by the corral was a river big enough to carry a big steamer. The river bank, which was at least fifteen feet straight up and down, made one wing of our corral.

One day my partner sacks out a big sunk-eyed bay colt, eases his saddle on him, bucks him out good and then tells me to open the gate. I opens the gate, and that bronk went past me like as if a wild cat was camped on his tail, in the next second he'd blind-bucked off the bank into the river and both him and the rider went out of sight in the whirling currents. They came up again about a hundred yards

In the next second he'd blind-bucked off the bank into the river.

down river and the horse, being cooled down some, begin to look for a way out. My partner was sure helping him, and down a few hundred yards more they made a landing where the stock had broke a run to water.

My partner rode him around some while I went to work on some of my bronks and then he unsaddled him. The next day that horse done the same thing, but my partner didn't go down with him that time, he quit the horse while he was still on land and let him go alone. We met the horse with a rope as he came out and my partner tried him again, he done the same thing and into the river he went once more, but this time we was going to give him plenty of that water. We'd tied a long rope to the hackamore before opening the corral gate, and when my partner quit him and the horse jumped off we held him there in one spot, where he had to swim or drown and where he couldn't climb out. When we got thru with him and towed him down to where he could get out that horse had enough water in him to last him a month. He never jumped in the river again.

But if that horse was cured of high diving into deep waters, he wasn't cured of blind-bucking and stampeding. That river jump-off was just one little spot in his young life and there was plenty of country left where it was scary for a rider to be on top of him.

I was always leary when my partner would ride that horse thru thick timber, he might stampede and leave him hanging on a limb sometime, with a broken neck, or while riding along the steep side of a tall mountain, it was awful long ways down and where missteps meant more than tumbles.

That horse did buck and stampede at them places, time and time again, and one day I sees my partner *walking* in at the corrals, his clothes was all tore and blood was all over him, but he was grinning, and I grinned too, in thinking the horse had finally killed himself.

But no such luck, the horse had stampeded and fell, my partner had held him down, tied him there so he couldn't move and left him.

"Thought I'd give him a little time to think about mending his ways," he says.

He left him tied down for a few hours. Quite a punishment for a horse, about the same, I guess, as locking a kid up and sending him to bed hungry. Anyway, the tying down sure worked on that horse and when my partner rode him the next day he seemed anxious to keep his eyes open as to where he was going and he never did buck blind again that I know of.

I had a blind bucker in my string about that time too. Mine and my partner's must of been related and that orneriness must of come from one strain. I got a strong hint of him being a blind bucker at the first saddling. I'd no more than took the foot rope off and stepped on him when he swapped ends acrost the corral and back like it was all open country. Every time he'd come to one side of the corral he'd hit it, like as if he couldn't see it, and near knock himself out sometimes. When I rode him outside the corral at the third or fourth saddling he'd bump against ten-foot boulders like as if they was pebbles, and once he bucked right into a deep washout with me and piled up in there. I got so I quit taking chances on that bronk, he sure wasn't responsible as to where he went nor as to how he landed. His ambition was to get rid of me and he didn't care how he skinned himself or if he broke his neck while doing that, so I didn't try to dicker with him much. I used a draw rein on him and if there was a tree handy, which there most always was, I'd do my best to steer him into it and make him bump his head. I always kept him on as level places as I could too and used another gate out of the corral instead of the one that led to the edge of the river. I can't swim and I don't like too much water, wether on a boat or on a horse.

I rode that horse for about two weeks I guess, off and on and while I was breaking others, and in that time I couldn't see where that horse was improving in his blind-bucking and stampeding, if he was improving it was for the worst. Then one day, being that the grub was getting low at camp I thought I'd ride him over to the trading post and supply up. I had to take a pack animal to bring the grub back on, and knowing that my horse might bust loose most any time and make me lose the lead rope I tied my pack animal to my horse's tail, and short. My pack animal was a little Spanish mule and didn't lead very well, and right there was where I stumbled onto a way to handle my narrow-brained blind-bucker. Every time he'd lose his head and start something that little mule would yank back and set down. She was kind of hard to budge too, and all my bronk could do was to jump up and down in one spot. When he was thru with his acting up the mule would come along then and lead pretty fair till he busted loose again, then she'd set down some more.

I'd have to laugh at both the horse and the mule. The horse would kick to break away from that drag on his tail and the mule would hang back to keep away from his heels. It worked fine both ways and my bronk didn't get the chance to buck away blind with me no time. By the time I rode him to the trading post and back, pulling that mule, that bronk seemed to get a little sense and got so he used his eyes some when he spooked.

Well, that was the beginning of the end of that bronk's blind-bucking. The next time I rode him I called on the mule to help me once again. I put a heavy rope around her middle, tied it down between her front legs, run one end thru the halter ring and tied it fast to the bronk's tail, that way the mule could hang back good and not get a sore neck. After a couple of saddlings, with dragging the mule around that way, my bronk had got so he'd quit spooking and losing his head. When I rode him a next time, without the mule, he behaved like an angel, and he never blind-bucked with me again. And the queer part afterwards is that that bronk got chummy with the mule, the two was together all the time, the bronk and his anchor.

It was a couple of years later when I seen that same bronk entered as a bucking horse at a rodeo. Somehow or other, after me and my partner turned all the bronks over as broke and got the okay on 'em, that one had went back to bucking again, and so good that he wound up as a contest horse. I was sure glad I didn't draw him, even if there was a tall arena fence to ride him inside of. I didn't use to mind a good hard honest bucker, but I never liked them that went blind on the job.

*Every time he'd lose his head and start something that
little mule would yank back and set down.*

"Once When the Laugh Was on Me"

I figger what makes a narrow escape such is not the danger that's in it so much as what a feller is in fear of most. Now for my part, there's two things that could always make chills run up and down my backbone, one is deep water and the other is height.

There's lots of folks such as them that works on sky scrapers and bridges that can perch themselves on near nothing up a couple of hundred feet in the air and look down to earth away below and feel as safe as any of the humans that's looking up at 'em. Then there's others that can make a fish blush for shame when it comes to swimming in the deep waters and diving from ungodly tall places.

I'm willing to give them kinds of folks all the credit, and sure won't crowd 'em in their liking for either the high places or the deep waters, and even tho the narrow escape I want to tell of here might sound kinda tame to some of 'em, it sure didn't leave no such impression with me.

This one happened in the water, and mighty cold water at that; there was still hunks of ice in it, and me being about as good a swimmer as the granite boulders that was in the bottom of that river is what hindered me considerable in grinning about it when it happened.

Me and a few other riders had just took a couple of thousand head of cattle on the summer range, a three days' drive, and we was coming back after another bunch. We was riding along at a pretty good gait, figgering on reaching the ranch before it got too dark.

A couple of miles or so from the ranch the boys strung out in a high lope and headed for the big bridge, I stayed behind thinking of taking a short cut and beating 'em to the ranch when they'd figgered I was still coming back of 'em. All went fine and the boys left me, remarking they'd see me in time for breakfast, then I turned to the right and headed my horse thru the cotton-woods of the river bottom in a high lope.

I'd crossed the river a few days before and remembered that it near made my horse swim then, and I'd forgot that it'd been raining pretty heavy since and raised the river up quite a few feet. It was a

I'd crossed the river a few days before.

treacherous river to cross at any time on account of the swift under currents, whirlpools, and boulders as high as the horse I was riding. There was holes washed out in places where the river would near hide itself under its own bank, and a feller had to be mighty careful in crossing to go straight ahead and not let the swiftness of the water get his horse swept along past the getting out place on the other side, or else both man and horse would have to swim on down the river a good mile before finding another landing place.

The banks was straight up and down on both sides and averaging eight and ten feet from the top to the water. I'd seen cattle drowned in that river pretty often, and noticed as I'd loped along trying to keep up with the critter so as I could pile my rope on 'er that there was no chance for anything but a fish in them waters when they was high—too swift. When a critter would hit one of them boulders she'd be turned over a half a dozen times, and then that same current would finally whirl 'er around and take 'er out of sight under the bank never to show up no more.

A cowboy had been drowned in that river a month or so before what I'm telling of happened; his horse finally got out of it somehow but that cowboy stayed in, and when the water went down that summer he was found buried in mud on a little island in the middle of it. One boot sticking up above the mud is all that told of his whereabouts.

But no thoughts of them happenings came to my mind as I made my horse take the water of that same river on the run. I was only thinking how I'd beat the boys in, turn my horse loose, and wait for 'em at the cook house. I was framing up what all I'd say to 'em when I heard the roaring of the swollen river fighting for a way over the big boulders, but even then I kept a loping along and heading straight for it plum forgetting what the last heavy rains had done since I crossed that river just a few days before. And it was pitch dark by then.

But it all came to me mighty quick as my horse jumped in, and then it was too late to turn back. My horse's legs was took right out from under him and he rolled over I don't know how many times. I had a heavy pair of chaps on, and a heavy coat, but none of that seemed to hinder me any when I realized what I'd jumped into.

I kicked my feet loose from the stirrups so I wouldn't be drug under and in the meantime I was making wild grabs for anything I

My horse's legs was took right out from under him and
he rolled over I don't know how many times.

could get a hold of. Nothing was handy for me to grab for quite a spell, and then just as I feel one of my hips connecting with a big boulder and I'm washed over past it, my fingers connect with long strands of hair. It was my horse's tail.

I sure hung on to that for I realized that if there was any way out that strong pony would sure find it. I'd lost all idea which way we was drifting but I did know we was sure making speed. The proof of that would come every time I'd come acrost a boulder, and then, of a sudden it seemed like all the water of that river was getting into my ears, nose, and mouth. Everything I'd done, good or bad, and from the time I was old enough to remember was run past in my mind, and all mighty clear; then came a time when I could hear little birds singing, and I could see big meadows all covered with flowers and the sun a shining for all it was worth. Everything was sure pretty and I don't know how long them thoughts and visions lasted but it seemed like for a long long time—then I didn't remember no more, till I looked up, and seen stars and stars galore, then with the noise of the roaring waters at my feet I could hear bellering cattle all around. I layed that way for quite a spell and must of went to sleep or something for when I looked up again a moon was shining. Then I come to and begin to move my head around.

I was laying in water up near to my chin and when I tried to move I found a lot of mud had been washed over me and I could hardly budge. I was feeling mighty weak and pretty well bloated up but soon as I thought a while and gathered up facts on what might happen if I layed there much longer, I sure worked hard to get out of there. What, I thought, if I couldn't pull myself out? The mud would keep on accumulating and gradually bury me, and then the water was rising.

That was all the spurring I needed, and from then on I wasn't satisfied to linger there no more, but getting out was a hard job and when finally I dragged myself away from under the mud and the edge of the river on up to higher and dry ground I just layed there till the sun came up and warmed me up to raise my head once more.

In my right hand I was holding part of my horse's tail which showed how I come to be on the edge of the river instead of in the middle. I'd hung on to that tail till my horse had got on the bank where he just kicked me loose and let me lay.

Some of the boys found me sometime later, and when I got so I could talk fairly well I told 'em how I'd tried to beat 'em to camp by crossing the river and taking a short cut.

"The laugh is on you Bill," says one of the boys.

But none of 'em seemed to take advantage of it, and for my part I'll sure as hell never forget it.

THE TURNING POINT

The last bucking horse I rode is, or was a couple of years ago, about as good a bucking horse as there was in the West, I could just as well say in the whole world because there's no fighting ponies nowheres than can come up with the western range horse of the U.S. on bucking ability that way.

Anyway, he was some bucking horse, and many a bronk rider would tell you so. We called him "Happy" because he looked anything else but that. His head was about as long as my arm, which is pretty fair length, and his body matched up with that head, but there the proportions ended, for his neck and legs was short and thick and didn't at all match with that head and body of his. I'd watch him graze once in a while and I'd have to laugh when I'd notice how, on account of his head being so long and his legs so short, he'd hardly have to bow his neck to reach for the grass. He was built like one of these Dutch hounds, two horse long and one horse high.

But that build of him was all a feller could find to grin at about that horse, and the minute a feller got up in the middle of him, all grins, if there was any, faded away, and a mighty concerned interest took place.

The way I come to meet up with this particular horse was very average, but what all he done to me wasn't at all average. —I'd come up from the deserts of southern Nevada, I'd been breaking horses for an outfit down there, and I'd got to feeling that being at a camp all by myself with them bronks, fifty miles from nowheres, didn't strike me as the best a feller could get out of life. If I'd had somebody to haze the bronks I was riding, and keep 'em out of the deep washes they'd run or buck into, things wouldn't been so bad, but there I was alone, and I was getting leery that I'd soon begin talking to myself.

Another thing is that I was getting fed up on breaking horses. The reckless feeling I'd had a few years before had received quite a few knocks and made my breath come short often. I'd got in a few mix ups with them ponies that left scars and broken bones to remind me, and as time went on and them mix-ups accumulated there'd come a day when, getting on an ornery horse, I noticed as I put my foot in the stirrup that my spur rowel was ringing. My whole left leg was shaking, and I begin to grin, but it was a kind of a serious grin, because to me the ring of that spur rowel was the same as a bell ringing that quitting time had come. I was getting nervous, or scared.

I was only twenty-six years old when I started to draw the line on the raw ones, and by then I'd spent many years on the backs of fighting ponies. I sat on my first horse when I was about four, and I remember 1900 as the year I got bucked off for the first time and was sent rolling down a hill. I was seven going on eight years old at the time, and I remember the year on account of my foster father buying me my first saddle, all for my own self.

With all the events that followed one another after that I felt by the time I was twenty-six that I'd sure enough done my share in the bronk-fighting game. By then my thoughts kept a going back to different happenings every time I'd climb onto a bowed-back horse, and when finally my spur rowels got to ringing a reminder of my lost nerve—was when I got to thinking of a job with gentler horses, a job where I'd get paid for being a cow-hand and not so much for being a bronk stomper.

I thought of hitting for Oregon, or some good range where there was trees and plenty of water. I wanted a change from the southern Nevada deserts, get a job from some big outfit, not as a bronk-peeler no more, but as an all-around cow-hand, and with a spread where I'd have the company of many riders.

It was while on my way that I met "Happy," that ill built black bucking horse I started telling about. He was the one that finally convinced me for sure that there was nothing in riding bad horses, and that it was high time for me to quit anyhow.

I'd come along to the town of Reno, Nevada. A big Rodeo was being pulled off there, and being I was just in time for the doings, I thought of maybe entering in the contest. But as my luck would have it, and I didn't kick about it, I fell into a steady job of hunting up some early-days' stage coaches for the stage-coach races, and chuck wagons for the same purpose, all to be used on the rodeo grounds. I had to do so much running around and was kept so busy at that that I didn't get to see only glimpses of the contest.

The rodeo lasted four days, and I'd got to meet many of the boys I'd knowed before, and from near every western state. I'd met a cowboy I rode with before the war, and natural-like him and me got to running together again; then us two run acrost another ranahan, and it was thru him that "Happy" and me got to mix.

Fred Conradt was this third feller's name. He started to break this "Happy" horse a few months before, and even tho Fred was a mighty good hand with a bronk, and a mighty good rider, him and that pony couldn't get to agree, and "Happy" would try to buck him off three or four times at every saddling. It seemed like that horse's ambition was natural-like against anything that had to do with being under a saddle, and the more Fred tried to make it easy for him the worse that pony got.

Then Fred, finally losing patience, had started to knocking on him. Maybe, he thought, that would bring the orneriness out of him, but it didn't, and even after a long day's ride that pony would tear things up just the same as if he'd just had a long rest. He'd got to buck so good that Fred begin to wonder often if he'd be able to stick on the next time.

Fred didn't stop to think about it while he was trying to make "Happy" behave that he was setting on a natural born bucking horse, a bad horse that'd always fight and never be good for anything but buck and tear things up. Good treatment had been tried on him to the limit, I know, because Fred likes horses too much to ever mistreat any of 'em, but this pony was just plain bad, just like you find a bad man sometimes amongst the best of people.

Them is the kind of ponies that go to make up the bucking horse strings that's shipped to all the big Rodeos like them that's held every year in such places as Chicago, Calgary, New York, Pendleton, and Cheyenne. They are the western range horses. Most of 'em are half-breds and big, fine looking horses, but being born and raised in the open, seldom seeing a human till they're four years old or more, they get every bit as wild as a deer, as strong and powerful as tho they was built of tempered steel, and as active and dangerous as a cornered tiger. When one of them horses is inclined to be bad, he is sure enough *bad* and no fooling.

"Happy" was turning out to be that kind. The more he was rode the more he got to know how to buck, and nothing else but. If while riding the hills Fred started him out after some bunch-quitting crit-ter that pony wasn't at all interested in heading 'er off, and instead he'd bog his head and make the cowboy buckle down to some real riding.

Fred rode that horse off and on for about a month, then work being over with that outfit for a spell, he turned him loose, caught up his private ponies and hit out for new range. Two months went by and then come time for the Rodeo, and after another month something came up which made Fred think of "Happy."

By that time me and Fred and this other feller I used to know before the war, his name is Elmer, we all got pretty thick, and the way the three of us kept together you'd think we was all handcuffed to one another. We never mixed with nobody else much unless it was some other cowboy, and we'd have the fun of our lives playing tricks amongst ourselves, and arguing about things that didn't amount to nothing.

It was while we was feeling rollicky that way one day that one of us suggested a little riding. Not riding along a path or nothing like that, but real riding, a good bucking horse or anything that was hard to set. Then, natural-like, Fred thought of "Happy." He got on his horse and rode out to get him, then two more horses was hunted up, one was "Hell-Morgan," a good bucker, and the other "Soleray," he was no slouch either.

"Hell-Morgan" was one of the buckers they'd had at the Rodeo, he done a good job there, and me being sort of fed up on bronk riding, and, as I said before, wanting to set on gentle horses for a change, I didn't crave so much for "Hell-Morgan" as a mount. I thought I'd like that long-bodied black best which Fred brought in. That was agreeable all around, so I drawed "Happy," Fred was to take "Hell-Morgan," and Elmer "Soleray."

The happenings that followed might go to show that when a feller makes up his mind to quit a thing he'd better do it or something most always happens which makes him wish he had. Of course I hadn't for sure made up my mind to quit as yet, but I'd thought about it and that amounted to the same thing.

Then again, and being I'd sort of figgered to leave rough horses alone, I'd got me a new saddle made. It was a saddle for roping and not so good for bronk riding. It was a full flower-hand-carved double rig, a daggone pretty little saddle and with a low fork and extra low cantle. The boys used to kid me about that cantle, saying all it was good for was to keep a feller from setting down. —I found that out.

And, to be real stylish, I'd ordered a pair of long twenty-six inch tapideros to go over the stirrups of that saddle and hang down. They're fine to work a herd with, but they're not so good on a bucking horse and I'd never rode one with tapideros before. Any rider will tell you that that's *some* disadvantage, specially with a stiff pair like mine was, and I figgered I was as much handicapped getting on a hard bucking horse with that outfit as Dempsey would be entering the fighting ring with gum boots on. —But being it was all for fun I didn't think about it.

This all might sound like a lot of excuses for what all goes on, and maybe it is, but I don't think there's anybody can face the sudden facts that he's a "hasbeen" without putting up some excuse about it, not if he's been in the game deep enough. And I still allow that I could of scratched that pony every jump he made if I'd had my old saddle, not that my old saddle was sure proof against getting throwed, because no such saddle can be made, but, if I do say it myself, no bronk got out from under me while I used that old "kak" and I'd rode and stomped some bronks in it that was as tough as "Happy" ever was. It was a kind of a slick rig too, but I knowed every inch of it—I knowed just how much room I had in it, and how loose I could ride without having it go from under me. And being I never rode on main strength, and never hung on a spur, I had to have *something* to go by which would give me a halfways even break with the horse I was riding.

With that new saddle, which was all different from the old one, I feel that "Happy" had all the advantage and me none, and I'll never forgive myself for getting on him so careless like, because that was the last hard horse I ever rode, and I'd sure like to feel now that I did ride that last one to a fare-you-well.

Anyway, as I slapped my new saddle on "Happy's" round back, I didn't think about no such a turning point as happened in my life a short while after.

I was the first rider up, and Fred done the snubbing while I done the saddling. I looked at them long tapideros the while and had a hunch I should take 'em off, but the hunch wasn't strong enough, and anyway I didn't want to take the time.

A blindfold over his eyes, "Happy" stood spraddle-legged and hardly moved. He was a true bucking horse, and he was saving all there was in him till the time come for him to put in his good work. And he was in mighty good shape to do that too, because it'd been three months since he'd been rode last, and all he'd had to do in that time was to feed up on tall bunch grass, get fat, and stack up on orneriness.

Fred didn't reckon on that then, neither did any of us, and we wouldn't cared anyway. So, as it was, and as Fred figgered, I was only getting on an average bucking horse, hard enough, but nothing special. He reckoned he'd be easy pickings for me.

I was the first rider up and Fred done the snubbing while I done the saddling.

We was all joking and grinning as usual when I eased my leg over the saddle and stuck my toe in the stirrup on the other side. "Happy" sort of squatted as I reached over and yanked the blindfold off his eyes, and then things started from there.

It was a wicked start, and the boys, as they told me afterwards, was just as surprised as I was. That pony seemed like to just blow up. He went up in the air from where he'd squatted, his head disappeared, and nothing was in sight but the saddle, which hit me from all sides and whirled as it hit.

Being I felt kind of rollicky myself, and was riding for fun, I had to laugh at the time on account of the confusion of things. That saddle seemed greased, and that little cantle at the back was all that kept me knowing of my whereabouts, only, sometimes it'd remind me too well and near knock me off. It'd pound me a few times and then it'd miss, and when I thought I was getting onto the hang of that pony's tactics he'd change 'em just that sudden and bring on new styles, but I kept track of that cantle some way and stayed straight up, even if I couldn't get lined out to riding.

Most horses when they first go to bucking bow their necks and make a long hard forward jump, but this "Happy" horse done just the opposite. He bowed his neck sure enough and ducked his head out of sight, but he didn't go forward and up, instead he went up and whirled backwards. He'd hit the ground as hard as he could and three or four times at each whirl, and each time backwards. He was what the bronk riders call a "spinner" and I was just beginning to realize that and ride according when he went to side-winding, then other ways which, far as I know, is not described by names.

I sure missed my old saddle thru all that commotion, but somehow I was having a lot of fun a trying to figger out the puzzle of sticking to this new one, and the deeper the puzzle got the more I

I sure missed my old saddle thru all that commotion, but somehow I
was having a lot of fun a trying to figure out the puzzle of sticking to
this new one, and the deeper the puzzle got the more I had to laugh.

had to laugh. I'd never seen myself ride in that style before, not since I was a kid.

Them long tapideros on my stirrups was some more for me to laugh at which sure kept me interested in trying to keep my feet inside of, for about the first thing that pony done as he whirled was to kick one plum off my foot, the wind had took the other, and there I was, foot loose, and setting on twelve hundred pounds of dynamite that kept exploding several times to the second.

I thought if I could get my feet inside them tapideros again and find the stirrups I could still put up a halfways decent ride, but them daggone long taps was just like a popper at the end of a whip, couldn't get a hold of 'em, and they kept a sticking up under my nose all the time and smacking me on one side and then another.

Being, as I said before, I wasn't much for hugging a horse or ride on main strength, I sure didn't have much to go by as to where and how I was setting. Everything was going up and snapping, even my shirt tail, all a whirling to hit hard and snap some more. Then seeing how I sure could never put up a ride without my stirrups that way, I went to trying to get 'em down from under my nose so I could put my foot in 'em. I grabbed the old nubbin (the saddle horn), a disgraceful thing for a bronk-peeler to do, but what could you expect of a has-been like me, and anyway, being I was riding for fun, I was going to grab it just long enough to get my stirrups—after that I was going to show 'em how riding is done.

But I didn't get to show off that way, because getting them daggone tapideros down where I could slip my feet inside of 'em was like trying to thread a fine needle with boxing gloves on your mitts while shooting the chutes.

But I was bound and determined to get my feet inside them taps if it was the last thing I ever done. I choked the nubbin a little more and went to fishing for 'em. "Happy" had done his worst by then, and I was sure leery he'd quit bucking entirely before I got them stirrups, because if he did, that sure wouldn't be no ride for me to be proud of. All on account of that strange saddle and them daggone tapideros too.

Thinking "Happy" was about ready to quit, one of the boys, Elmer, rode up alongside of me and asked between jumps if I wanted him to "pick up." I laughed at him and never answered, for I was still in hopes of getting my stirrups and putting up some sort of a ride before the horse was ready to quit.

But I was too late now. Gradually, "Happy's" head begin to come up, the hard hitting jolts eased up to long easy crowhops, and I knowed that any minute his head would come up all the way and he'd go to stampeding with me. Now was the time to quit him, before he started to run, because he was heading for a patch of heavy timber, and what would happen to me in there on top of that horse would be left for the pine limbs to tell.

There was nothing for me to do now but step off, for the ride, as bum as it was, was over. There was no use looking for stirrups no more, so I sort of eased to one side figgering to throw my leg over the horse's neck as he went and let him go out from under me. But glancing ahead a little to make sure of my footing, I got a glimpse of a railroad track, and then I thought of sticking on a little longer. I didn't want to take no chances of stumbling on that.

It was about then that something happened, and it was all on account of me getting set to step off and then changing my mind. "Happy" had felt me easing to one side, and being the wise horse he was, he took advantage of it. He brought a crooked hard hitting jump of the kind he'd started out with, and it felt to me like he'd stuck both feet in a badger hole that had no bottom to, of a sudden, hit solid bedrock, and me being set to step off instead of being set to ride I sure wasn't prepared for no such. I was throwed hard and landed in a heap between the railroad tracks, my head hit one of the rails, "Happy" planted one foot in the middle of my back and went on, then I didn't know no more.

The boys told me afterwards how they was sure scared that I was a dead one. They said I was all twisted, chest down, face up to the sky, and half of my scalp tore up and hanging over the rail.

But I fooled 'em, and after they straightened me up, and got air in my lungs, it wasn't long when I begin to grin at 'em— The first thing I thought of was how I'd spoiled the fun by going to work and getting hurt, and I figgered on making up for that in a way so it wouldn't strike 'em as very serious. I went on grinning, started to brush the dirt off my clothes unconcerned like, and even went to singing an old song the cowboys all know, "Bury me not on the lone prairie."

A little crowd had gathered around by then, and one feller hearing me sing, remarked, "He's out of his head."

"You'd be out of your head too," I come back at him, "if you'd tried to bend a railroad track with it."

The boys kidded me about that for a long time afterwards and said that the railroad company was going to sue me for damages, but they wasn't kidding much when the accident happened, and I couldn't fool 'em none as to how bad I was hurt. Blood was streaming down from my head plum down to the toe of my boots, and after trying to put all the hide back in place over that dome of mine, somebody around who had a car was kind enough to offer to take me to a doctor.

That was the wind up of the last bucking horse I rode. I felt the effects of that for a couple of years afterwards on account that during that last ride an old internal injury had been stirred, and it begin to bother me again.

And that's how come I didn't go to Oregon, as I'd first planned. "Happy" had proved to be my turning point, a mighty rough one maybe, but my turning point sure enough. While I was recuperating I happened to think of a mining man I'd met who said he'd give me a grand letter of introduction to an editor of a magazine on the west coast. This mining man knowed the editor well, and being he'd seen some of the drawings I'd made and which I'd packed 'round from cow camp to cow camp, he'd thought I was foolish not to try and get some of that work in the magazines and make a living that way instead of riding.

I didn't pay no serious attention to that man's good advice right then, most likely if I hadn't met up with "Happy" I'd forgot all about it, and right to-day I'd still be riding for a living—not that I'd mind that so much, but this ain't so bad either, and being a has-been I'd rather draw and write about that life than take a back seat as a rider.

So, if I'm to be thankful, "Happy" is the one who'd get the first thanks. He's the one who jolted the mining man's advice back to my memory, and fixed me so I'd have time to think about it afterwards. He's the one that showed me for sure that I'd rode one too many bronks, and that it was high time for me to quit and be sensible.

I often thought about that afterwards, and when I bought my little outfit here in Montana and had Fred come up to run it for me, I wanted to get "Happy" and turn him loose amongst the tall grass of my best range, and just have him to look at as a reminder. But Fred tells me that "Happy" got valuable after I left the cow country and hit for the art world. He tells me, and so does a few other riders, that "Happy" made a big name for himself amongst the Rodeo bucking horses, maybe not as big a name as some of 'em did, but he was as good as any, and bucked his man off as often as the best of 'em.

And come to think about it, that careless ride I put on "Happy" proved to be his turning point too, because up till then there was talks of putting him in the harness and breaking him to work. "Happy" would of been pulling a wagon for the rest of his life, and I know that wasn't his calling because he put too much heart in his bucking.

The next year I was pushing a crayon in my rope hand and making pictures of bucking horses and such for the magazines. In the summer of that same year "Happy" was entered as a bucking horse at a big rodeo and when he come out of the chute he bucked his rider off in the first jump. That rider was a good one too, he'd rode many hard buckers and qualified high at many contests, but when he came out on "Happy" that day he didn't get nowheres, and he was heard to say afterwards that he'd never seen so many horses at one time as he seen in that black horse.

Off and on I'd hear some more about "Happy's" bucking ability. He got to be a wanted horse at many a rodeo thru Northern California and bucked many a good man off. Good riders who'd come from far and near to compete for the prize money that was offered, and these men was serious in their riding, they didn't straddle "Happy" nor none of the buckers with no low forked, low cantle, roping saddle, and there was no tapideros on their stirrups to interfere with their riding; but "Happy" bucked many of 'em off just the same, and as I heard it often, about every other man fell by the wayside when they came out of the chute on that horse.

"Happy" was right in the thick of what he was cut out for. It was an art with him, the same as it is with any good bucking horse—he was born to it. He kept a going up at that game, and then one day I heard that he was in the bucking string at the Pendleton round up, one of the biggest contests in the world and at such an event where none but the world's fightingest bucking horses are gathered.

"Happy" had reached the top of the ladder as a bucking horse, and he was at the same standing a prize fighter was when under Tex

That same year "Happy" was entered as a bucking horse at a big rodeo, and
when he come out of the chute he bucked his rider off in the first jump.

Rickard's wing, only maybe not as profitable— But "Happy" didn't care, not as long as he could buck a man off.

I was mighty glad, and sort of proud, at hearing of "Happy's" high standing as a bucking horse, because I feel that I had a lot to do in the turning point in that pony's career, and also mine, because if it hadn't been for him maybe I wouldn't be writing and drawing about him to-day. We was more or less one another's object which turned us from aimless ramblings to the way our natural talents pointed; and now, somehow, I don't feel so bad for getting on that horse with a saddle that gave him all the advantages.

I don't feel so bad that I'm a has-been, that I put up such a bum ride, and was hindered with them long tapideros, on the last bucking horse I straddled, because now I see where providence played a hand, and some day I'd like to see "Happy" again, and I'd like to touch his black hide in a sort of a handshake from one artist to another— But sometimes, as I feel the scar that runs over the top of my head, I do wish I'd had my old saddle that day when I straddled "Happy."

Up in the Eagle Territory

Of the "tight squeezes" I've had that's in my memory to stay there's one I like to remember on account that it's past and left away behind, and right to-day when I think of it I feel a sort of cool breeze running up and down my backbone. *I was there* and the main character at the doings.

To the folks that's had no dealings or rode the ponies that's handed the cowboy in the cow countries this experience I've had and want to tell of might sound as average, and being I'd hate to see anybody go through the same so as to get the feeling, I'll go to work and do a little explaining.

Imagine if you can that you're riding a big stout ornery horse with a neck on him a foot thick and so stiff that it could hardly be bent with a block and tackle; on the end of that neck is a head that looks more like a hundred pound sledge hammer and shows about the same feeling. The only way you can turn him is to biff him alongside of the ear with your hat, and about that time he goes to bucking and stampedes away with you.

That's all that horse wants to know is buck, stampede, get you in a pinch and kill you if he can, and so spooky that every time you try to roll a cigarette on him, or even spit, he'll bog his head and make you ride for all you're worth. Them big twelve hundred pound ponies can make riding pretty rough too.

And don't anybody think I'm at all exaggerating on the horse I'm *trying* to describe; the cowboy finds plenty of just that kind on every outfit he hires out to ride for, and some worse. There's no possibility of ever exaggerating on how a range bronc can act.

"Spooks" is the name of the hammer-headed pony I'm telling of; when he was a colt he'd bucked into a hornet's nest with a feller and kept a bucking at every little excuse since. The shadow of a bird on the ground was enough to get him started, and a hornet or deer fly

The only way you can turn him is to biff him alongside of the ear with your hat.

hanging around his nose was sure to make him act up. He'd strike at 'em and go to bucking from there, and the way he could reach your spurs with his hind feet didn't make things at all comfortable for the rider that was on him.

But he was a good horse and no ride was too long for him; he'd be just as ready to buck with you after a hard day's work as he was when first saddled. I had him buffaloed a little and behaving pretty fair in good country, but when we'd be where the land was cut up and rough and steep I think he had *me* buffaloed a little too, and he sure knowed it. I never did like the thought of what that pony would do to me once he'd got me in a pinch.

103

And that's where my experience comes in; he finally did get me in a pinch, and I figger all that saved me was that he'd got himself in the same pinch too; he was sure careful with his own hide.

I was riding that horse on circle one morning—it was during the spring round-up. Tracks on the sandy trail leading up into the Bad Lands was the cause of me turning my horse and going after the stock that'd left the signs. I started out after 'em on a high lope till the climb got Spooks to wanting to slow down some, and as the trail was narrowing fast I let him.

We pegged along on a dog trot for quite a ways and the trail kept a getting narrower; the cattle had left it but I figgered they'd be on top of the pinnacle and the best way to get there was to follow the trail I was on. We crossed a few bad spots and as the trail got higher and steeper and narrowed I noticed that Spooks was getting ticklish and "scared at his tail" for no excuse; he was getting even with me for the way I'd make him behave on the flats. I couldn't spin him around up there on that trail or set him where I wanted him, and he knowed it.

We was up amongst the eagle territory and a long ways down to flat ground and that daggone horse was taking it out on me by acting like he was going to stampede any minute and go to bucking down into "China." The trouble was, I knowed he was fool enough to do it, which made me feel at times like I wanted to be a little bird and just fly away. It was a mighty good country for birds up there, and goats too.

I was making myself as small as possible and kept mighty quiet as we kept a going up and up; I was handing pet words to that horse while at the same time I was wishing I had him down in decent country where I could take the kink out of him.

But the worst was yet to come and I sure realized it at a glance as I looked on the trail ahead. The spring waters had washed out a big gash on the face of the cliff; it'd took out six feet off the trail and where that trail resumed again on the other side it was about two feet higher which made it all mighty hard to jump.

To a trained jumping horse it would of been easy enough, *maybe*, but the range bronc is not much on jumping except when he's bucking and besides that little six foot jump which might of been cleared easy on level ground sure looked a heap different; it seemed wider, deeper and yawning a heap, away up there. I couldn't take a run at it on account that the narrow space my horse was on called for a lot of care as to where each foot was put.

I noticed all that at a glance, and seen there was nothing for me to do but ride on to where I had to stop, and that came soon enough. Spooks realized quicker than I did that here was a place where he could sure put in his bluff and scare the life out of me, and he done a fine job. He stood there for a minute sizing up everything that was to his advantage; he snorted and shook himself and started rearing up, and all the while I only wanted him to stand so I could figger a way past the bad place.

There was no turning back, for as it was there was only about two feet of trail to stand on and on both sides of us was straight up and *down*, for a couple of hundred feet. I couldn't even get out of my saddle on account that, as it was, my right leg was plumb up against the bank, and if I'd ever tried anything like getting off of him right then that pony would of found it a mighty nice chance to kick the belly off of me; it was on the wrong side to get off, too, the injun side.

I think I prayed there for a while, and while Spooks was acting up and showing indications that he was going to start down any second I was studying the bank on the other side and wondering if my horse could jump it whether it would hold him or not; but I had no choice and thought I'd better try it before that horse got it into his head to start flying down off our perch.

I showed him the trail as best I could and let him snort at the opening he had to jump. Just then a little hornet started buzzing and I didn't want to think what would happen if that daggone hornet ever got near Spooks's nose; instead I acted. I showed the horse the trail once again and then I touched him with the spur.

He snorted and shook himself and started rearing up.

He let out a snort but behaved pretty good till he come to where he had to make the jump, and there he stopped sudden, so sudden the earth started giving out from under him, and we was starting to slide over the edge.

By some miracle he caught himself and then I felt kinda weak all at once. I never could stand height. We both stood there and shivered for a spell and when my heart slowed down to a walk once again, I begin to see red. I was getting peeved clear thru at the idea of that fool horse getting funny at such a place.

From then on I made that horse think I had him on a big flat, and I started him acrost with no light persuading. That sure took him by surprise and when it come time for him to jump he sure never hesitated; I didn't give him time to. He stretched out like a flying squirrel and sailed over to the other side, his front feet connected with solid earth but his hind ones didn't have no such luck.

I wasn't peeved no more right about then, I was just plain scared and my heart went up my throat. There was no foolishness left in that big horse just that minute either, he worked and clawed and every time the dirt would give away from under one hind foot another would come up and get a new hold till it seemed like there'd be no end to it.

The big horse was gradually going further back and loosing ground at every lunge he'd make, and he was taking me with him—I had a good chance to jump off of him right then and be sure of getting good footing but that never come to my mind, and I knowed that my weight on his withers was all that was saving him from falling straight over backwards into nowheres.

Spooks realized that, I know, and he was putting up a game fight. He was still trying when most ponies would quit and go down; and finally, when all hopes seemed past the big bay horse let out a squeal and tore at the earth with his hoofs till it shook all around. I felt his back muscles working even under my saddle and then, all at once his hind feet found solid earth.

We went on a ways till the trail broadened out some and we seen clear sailing ahead; then I got out of my saddle and loosened up the cinches so as to give him a good chance to breathe. Spooks was sure taking advantage of it and he didn't seem to mind when I run my hand along his neck.

"Little horse," I says as I rubs him back of the ears, "you may be a dam' fool, sometimes, but you've sure got guts."

Down the Wash

It always struck me sort of queer how sometimes things can happen when they're the least expected or thought of, and when just being able to live and navigate around seems the greatest privilege in the world something just seems to drop out from under you and of a sudden you're in a fix where you begin to count the minutes you've got left to live in. . . . It seems to me there ought to be some sort of warning so a feller can kind of prepare, or dodge, if he can.

I was riding along one day whistling a tune, my horse was behaving fine and all was hunkydory and peaceful. Ahead a ways I'd noticed a narrow washout and I kept on a riding. I'd rode over many a one of them, and nothing was there to warn me that I should go around this perticular one.

My horse cleared the opening and I was still a whistling, then, of a sudden my whistling stopped short as I felt the earth go out from under my horse's feet, . . . the next thing I know I was in the bottom of a ten-foot washout and underneath twelve hundred pounds of horseflesh.

I was pinned there to stay, and lucky I thought afterward that my whole body wasn't underneath that horse. It could of just as well been that way, only past experiences with horses had saved me and natural instinct had made me try to stay on top of the horse whether he was upside down or right side up. As it was, I was kind of on the side of him, my head was along his neck and only my left hip and leg felt the pinch of the weight.

The washout was only about three feet wide, at the bottom, just enough room for me and that horse to get wedged in nice. The old pony was fighting and bellering and kicking big hunks of dirt down on top of us. I was kinda worried that he might undermine the bank of the washout and have it cave in on us and bury us alive so I grabbed his head and hugged it toward me thinking that would quiet him down and keep him from tearing things up so much. I figgered that if there'd be any squeezing done it would be on the other side, for as it was I sure had no room to spare.

Well, he fought on for quite a spell, then he laid still for a while. If that horse had been good and gentle I could of maybe got him to lay still long enough so I could try and dig myself out with my hands, but just as soon as I'd move to try anything like that he'd let out a snort that sounded mighty loud in that perticular place and go to fighting again.

His hoofs would start flying and tearing things up and what little dirt I'd scraped away with my fingers would be replaced with a few

I'd rode over many a wash like it and I didn't see why I should go around this perticular one.

hundred pounds of the side of the washout. I was having a mighty hard time keeping my head clear and out in the air and the dirt kept accumulating and piling up on top of us till there was nothing but part of the horse's legs, still a going, and our heads sticking out.

Then it comes to me that if that horse keeps on a kicking and bringing down more dirt he'd soon be in a fix where his legs would be all buried and he'd have to be still, but I was sure worried about a big hunk of overhanging dirt he might loosen up while doing that. It looked like it weighed at least five tons and I didn't want to think of it dropping down on us.

There was one way where I could win out, and that was to dig for my six-shooter which it was lucky was on my right hip and possible to get at. With that six-gun I could shoot the horse, there'd be no more dirt coming down and I could easy enough dig myself out with the same gun, and I could take my time about it too.

That was one way and the best one, but I sure didn't want to shoot that horse and decided I wouldn't till I just had to save him from suffering. Shooting a horse wasn't appealing to me even in the fix I was in. It would of saved my carcass for sure but I was finding more pleasure in looking for other ways out than just that one.

I kept my eye on the hunk of dirt above my head, and while the pony by me would have another fit once in a while and small piles of dirt would keep a coming down I was finding my breathing capacity getting smaller and smaller. My body was beginning to feel numb from my chest on down and I felt that the only part of me that was living was from my chest on up.

I thought of the boys I started out from camp with that morning and wondered *when* they'd miss me and start looking for me, and then once again I thought of my six-gun. If I could get it out and fire a shot once in a while some of 'em would maybe hear.

I'd been digging pretty steady and with just the idea of keeping my right arm and head clear. I knowed that I couldn't get away even if all the dirt was off—the horse was on me and holding me down, but from then on I wanted my gun and I sure went to work for it.

It took me a good hour's time to get it out and my gloves was wore to a frazzle, but I finally managed it, and soon as I shook the dirt out of the barrel I held it straight up and fired. The shot echoed along the washout and sounded like it could be heard for many miles. I waited and listened for an answer and then I noticed where the sun was. It was slanting in where me and my pony was getting buried alive and it was making things all the hotter down there.

By it I figgered it was along about noon, all the boys excepting me would be back to camp from the first "circle" and wouldn't be starting out again for a while. I was about ten miles from camp and when they would start out again I knowed they'd go another direction as all the cattle in the country I was at was run in that morning. The shot I had fired had been for nothing.

Riders was often late getting in with cattle and I knowed they hadn't thought anything had happened to me as yet. I also knowed they wouldn't think anything was wrong till that evening when they gathered in to eat, and till then I thought was an ungodly long time to wait.

And what was more, how was they going to find me if they did start looking. I was sure well hid and they'd have to pretty near know the exact spot where I was located, I could make a noise with my gun of course. . . . All them thoughts was mighty cheerful thoughts not to have, but I couldn't dodge 'em. If only that big ton of dirt above my head hadn't been so threatening things would of been easier, but there it was as big as death and I couldn't take my eyes from it.

The sun was slanting in where me and my pony was getting buried
alive and it was making things all the hotter down there.

Finally the sun left us. It was going on west to its setting point and left me still doing some tall thinking. The big horse alongside of me was quiet for good—the dirt had piled up on top of him till his toes disappeared and he *had* to be still. But his breathing wasn't very good to listen to so close to my head, and I didn't find it at all inspiring as to ways and means of getting out of there.

Clods of dirt would still keep a falling off and on but there was signs of 'em quitting since the horse had got quiet. It was too late for me to try to dig out though, but I was still at it and at the same time watching that I didn't tickle or jar the side of the bank that held the all-powerful heavy piece of earth.

As I worked and clawed at the dirt and wished for badger claws instead of bleeding fingers I found that my resting spells was coming oftener and stayed longer. It was just as the sun was going down and when I'd took an *unusual* long rest that I realized I was holding something in my hand that I'd grabbed a hold of when I was ready to quit. It was a clump of rabbit brush that'd fell in from the top with the dirt that'd got loosened—more of it was a hanging up there.

My hand was on my chest as I studied where that piece of brush had come from. I felt a chill run up and down my backbone as I realized that it'd come from no other place than the big hunk of over-hanging dirt. *It was loosening up.*

The thought of that near had me moving, my hand closed in on my shirt just for something to grab a hold of, and as I did that I felt something breaking in my shirt pocket. It was matches.

I held my hand there for a while and done some thinking. I noticed the clump of rabbit brush my hand was still holding and then I looked up ten feet above to where there was lots of the same brush hanging over the edge.

I couldn't think so very fast along about then and I only realized it was dark when I lit a match and it throwed a light, but the rest of the programme didn't need no thinking—everything was in front of me to follow and that's what I did.

I held the match under the piece of rabbit brush I had and it took holt and flamed like that kind of brush does. When I thought the flame was strong enough to stand a little breeze I heaved it as best I could up toward the other brush ten feet above me.

The first attempt wasn't much good, the little piece of brush came back on me, singed me a little and then died. I tried it again and finally landed it up amongst the brush along the top of the bank. Then I held my breath.

A little flame shot up and throwed a light on the opposite side of the washout. I watched that and seen where the flame seemed to gradually die down. "If that fire don't start," I says out loud, "I'm just as good as done for," which was the truth.

But it did start, slow and aggravating but sure, and pretty soon it gets lit up above, and I can see the sparks fly and some of 'em are falling down on me and the horse but it was sure good to see that light and hear that brush a roaring in flame. I knowed what rabbit brush would do once it got started to burning, I knowed it'd spread and throw a mighty good light for as long as any of that kind of brush was around. And if I remembered right, that kind of brush was plenty thick along that wash for a good mile or so.

From then on instead of digging I put my efforts to waiting and that was getting to be some painful too, but my hopes had went up a lot since I got such a good signal fire started. I felt sure somebody would ride up and look for me soon, and sure enough, after a while I hear somebody holler, my six-shooter barks out an answer and then I thinks, . . . what if somebody should ride up on that piece of country that's hanging over me and just waiting for some little weight to start it down.

The thought of that sure got my lungs to working. . . . "Stay back," I hollered, "stay back."

"Where are you, Bill," somebody asks.

"In the bottom of the washout," I answers, "but don't come near the edge of where I'm at or it'll cave in—get in from some other place."

I didn't have to tell them to hurry, they was doing that a plenty and pretty soon half a dozen riders was digging me out with running irons, six-shooters, and everything they could get hold of that'd scatter the dirt. The horse was lifted off of me and I was pulled out to where I could work my legs and get the blood to circulating in 'em.

It took four saddle horses to pull my horse out and straighten him up to stand, and by the time I got through telling the boys what happened, how it happened and all I felt half-ways strong enough to stand up again. With the help of one of the boys I walked over to investigate the hunk of earth that'd been hanging over me and threatening me all that long day. There was a crack in the ground and back of it which showed how ready it was to fall. I stuck my boot heel in that crack and shoved a little, and about that time I was pulled away.

The earth seemed to go out from under us as that hunk left, a big cloud of dust went up, and when we looked again the washout was near filled to the top.

Wound Up

In the cowboy's work and of the many things that causes him to act mighty quick at times, there's nothing that can compete with the rope, nothing, unless it's a bronc's four feet. That long, far-reaching string of whale line with a loop at the end can find more ways of coming back at the man that throws it than anything I know of. It can sail out as pretty as you please, settle over a critter's horns, and upset 'er to lay in a good tying position. Ninety-nine times out of a hundred it does that for the man that can manipulate it well, but even with the good roper there comes times when that plain and harmless looking hard-twist-manila turns like a snake and quicker than lightning, circles around the cowboy's body and near cuts the life out of him before he can even see it come.

Folks might wonder what could make a innocent little rope be so wicked as to act that way, and the explaining is not easy, but— First, it's the horse you're roping off of, he don't always behave, and then again he might be just a raw bronc unedicated to the ways of the rope. Second, is the steer the loop has slipped up onto, he's got lots of wild weight and he don't know that a rope has an end, so, when he hits that end while going full speed ahead is when something always does bust.

If all's well the steer will be the one to "lay," but sometimes the horse and rider does the laying stunt instead, and that's what leads to things happening, happening too fast for the eye to follow. . . . There's where the little rope comes in, then's when she does her winding, and when all's over and the dust settles again there's neat rope burns which for a long time afterwards keeps reminding. . . . But that ain't all a rope can do, she has many other tricks which keeps the cowboy's eye and hand on the slack.

Like one day for instance, me and Hippy Darrell was on "circle" and as usual, combing the range for whatever stock we'd see. We'd rounded up quite a little bunch and was headed for camp with 'em when from our left comes a sudden streak of dust. What made it was headed straight for us and pretty soon we could make out the shape of a steer. He kept a coming, and as we watched we could see by his actions that he was on a rampage. Something had sure stirred him up, and as he joined the cattle we was driving in he never seemed to notice us none at all. His head was high and he was seeing red, and somehow with that pair of long well-curved horns he was packing he was sure good to look at.

Hippy edged up to within speaking distance, and grinning, he remarked, "Somebody's turned him once too often."

"Yep," I agrees. "It don't take much to make 'em want to fight sometimes, and a feller often has so many to handle that he can't tend to these 'bunch quitters' as he'd want to."

Being on the "prod" (fight), the big steer didn't care whether us riders was within a yard or a mile of him, so long as we didn't stand in his way or try to turn him. He stayed in amongst the cattle we was driving till he kind of got his second wind, and from then on he begin to find fault, the bunch was going too slow, and besides they wasn't going the right direction for him. He begin going back and forth through the bunch. Once in a while he'd go out of it only to come back again and kept that up till, instead of cooling down to behaving, his fighting spirit stayed up to the boiling point and edged him on to do everything but what seemed right and natural.

We left him alone. If he went out of the herd we'd let him come back by himself and tried not to let on that we was driving him along, but no matter what he done we was going to take that big boy in to the "cutting grounds" where all the cattle of that morning's circle was gathered. It's the rule at all times that every hoof is brought in, and no cowboy ever lets anything get away that he sees unless something happens that he just can't.

The big steer had went out of the bunch about a half a dozen times and each time he'd stop, and soon as he found there was nobody around to turn him he'd then turn of his own accord and come back to the herd. We looked for him to quiet down, but it seemed like he had no such intentions, and he'd got us to the point where we wanted to stretch our ropes on him and roll him over a few times, just to sort of give him all the trouble he was looking for and a little edication to boot.

He went out once more, and the way he held his head, curved his backbone, and kinked his tail all a challenging, we knowed he wasn't figgering on coming back no more.

Hippy looked at me and grinned, and I grinned back. Two shakes and our ropes split the air into loops, our spur rowels tickled our ponies' flanks and in a short while we was within roping distance of our bunch-quitting steer.

The horse I was riding wasn't even what you'd call half broke, I couldn't get him to line out straight ahead like Hippy could his. Hippy was riding a well-broke horse and even though he was ornery at times he sure savvied the cow, so that's how come that the first rope that sailed over the big steer's horns was Hippy's, and all was done so quick and neat that the steer didn't know there was a cow-boy near him till he felt hisself lifted off the earth and jerked down to lay. His head was at the place his tail had been and it didn't take half a second to make the change.

All would have been well, and Mr. Steer's senses would of been jarred back to behaving normal again, but just at the wrong time Hippy's horse started to fighting his head which caused the rope to slack up. In another second the steer was up, and bleary-eyed looks us over.

Hippy was just about to take another fall out of the steer when that horse of his bogged his head and went to bucking. It was then that I tried to get the steer to put his attention on me, but he seemed more interested in Hippy and the bucking horse, and knowing what the slack of a rope would do in the mix up of a bucking horse and a mad steer I done my best to keep the steer away and the rope tight. But that daggone wall-eyed critter had other intentions, and after making a pass at my horse with his long horns he let out a beller and

Two shakes and our ropes split the air into loops.

headed straight on for Hippy and the bucking horse he was trying to make behave.

I let my rope sail as he went by and a neater throw never was made, the loop made a perfect circle as it was about to settle over the steer's horns, and being so sure that I had him is what spoiled my catch. I pulled up my slack a shade too soon and instead of catching two dangerous horns I caught a lot of air.

From then on things happened too fast for me to build another loop and make another throw. There was a mixture of steer, horse, horns, winding ropes, and a man. Natural like I thought of my six-shooter, but I never drawed it on account that Hippy was so much everywheres and seeming like all at once. I wondered what made him hang on when he should of quit, and right about then I noticed something that made me lose my tan. . . . Two wraps of the rope

There was a mixture of steer, horse, horns, winding ropes, and a man.

was around Hippy's waist, he was tied to the saddle, and what scared me still more was how I seen the saddle was slipping and getting on the horse's side.

I'd often told Hippy to start a smudge with that damned centre-fire rig and get hisself a real saddle, and right then I wished I'd done it for him, but it was too late to worry about that at that time. I sat on my horse feeling like a daggone fool cause I didn't do anything, but there was nothing I could do, not a thing. I could only watch for a chance, and that much I was sure doing.

The steer was going around and around and trying to get a solid dig with his horns. I could of shot him easy enough, but it'd made things a lot worse on account that his dead weight on the rope against the live weight of the horse would of sure made a heavy drag on the rope, and being that rope was around Hippy's waist he'd sure been cut in two.

Finally a break came, which right then seemed to me for even worse. The steer while circling around the horse and trying to get his horns to working had connected with that pony's hoofs and his nose had been pounded on till there come a time when he figgered it'd be best to leave that horse and man have it out by themselves. He made another jab with his horns and missing went right on for the open country. He went on for about thirty feet, the length of rope that was left, and when he hit the end that was still around his horns he hit it so hard that it took his head and feet away from him and he was stretched on his side.

That sudden jerk daggone near took the horse off his feet but as luck would have it the rope had tightened just when he was close to the ground instead of being up in the air. The jerk of the rope never interrupted him none at all and instead he seemed to buck all the harder.

I got a glimpse of the saddle being jerked from the side of the horse till it went under his belly, and still fastened to it by two wraps of the rope which near cut him in two was Hippy, and in the worse place a man could be. His head and arms was under the horse's chest, and his legs was dragging on the ground while it looked like that ornery pony was reaching under with his hind legs and kicking that cowboy to pieces.

I sort of wanted to close my eyes for a second for I thought sure Hippy was going to be kicked and dragged into scattered remains, but my eyes didn't close none at all. Instead, and in less time than it takes to tell it I was off my horse, had my knife out, and luck being with me for once I got a holt of the rope. . . . I never seen such a hard rope to cut as that one seemed to be right then. I whittled at it and was jerked around a trying to keep a holt of it till I thought my eye teeth would jar loose, but finally she came apart, the two thousand pounds of earth tearing critter and horse-flesh was separated and the coils that'd wrapped around Hippy's waist let go.

The cowboy slipped to the ground and the wild pounding hoofs of the bucking horse barely missing him went on over leaving him, clothes half tore off, his body all twisted, and looking like dead.

I straightened him out quick as I could and to looking like human again, and I was sure some surprised to find after tallying up on where and how bad he was hurt that with all the rope marks around his waist, a few bruises and a busted ankle there was nothing about him that wouldn't heal up again.

It was a couple of days later when passing by where Hippy was laying in the shade of the chuck-wagon and recuperating that that cowboy hollered at me and says:

"Say Bill, I thought you knowed better than cut a good rope in the centre and spoil it like you did mine, you could of just as well cut it by the hondoo and saved it, couldn't you?"

I never seen such a hard rope to cut as that one seemed to be right then.

A STAMPEDER

Of all the happenings that's apt to make a cowboy white around the gills there's none that averages up with a stampeding horse, a horse that gets scared of his tail or his shadow and goes to bucking and running away blind. Not much of the cow country is level and I know of lots of it where you'd have to go some to keep your horse going faster than a walk. There's cliffs a hundred feet straight up, steep mountain sides a mile high and covered with fallen timber, big boulders, and all cut up with wash-out ravines that can't be seen for brush. A stampeding bronk in such places is going to warm up the coolest of riders.

I had a horse break away with me in a particular bad place one time. Not once did he look where he was going, instead he was looking back at me and snorting and kicking with every jump. I was the one that was doing the looking ahead, and every time I tried to bust him up the mountain he'd go to fighting his head. That old mountain was sure steep and I thought every second that my horse would roll over. Then I seen a big cut ahead, and we was heading straight for it.—Right now, I figgered, was a good time for me to dissolve partnership with the old pony. I knowed better than to set down on one rein and try to turn him because in such a place that would only caused him to fall; all I could do was to steady him and quit him soon as possible. I was just preparing to leave him when about then something happened which sure made me change my mind and stick to the old saddle for all I was worth. We'd brushed up against a pine tree and one of the twisted dry limbs had slipped through the stirrup, broke and stuck there. It had wedged my foot in as pretty as you please, and I couldn't pull it out, one end of the stick was prodding my horse to doing even worse than ever before. He was running too fast to buck well but he was sure doing his daggonedest to do both, and he was more than scattering things.

He was looking back at me and snorting and kicking at every jump.

The way it was now it sure looked as if the Good Lord from up above or the devil from down below had fixed things so I'd be due to be registering with one of them soon. I had less than a hundred yards to ride to reach the cut, and there is where I figgered would come the sudden end. I couldn't quit my horse for fear of my foot hanging in the stirrup, and, if it had to be, I'd rather fall to a death than be drug to it.

I done my best to stick and stared at my grave which now was not many yards away; then my horse fell—he'd come acrost a fallen tree which he didn't see—and as he fell I lost my saddle, my foot stuck in the stirrup, and, as the pony rolled over and over, I was wrapped around him just like I was so much string.

It's sure queer how sometimes a feller will miss a thousand bumps when at other times he'll connect with one lonely jolt which queers him. Well, I missed many bumps in that fall and I was in the thick of 'em. I was rolling around with a thousand pounds of horse flesh and striking hoofs, amongst jagged boulders and bayonet-like pine limbs. We rolled on that way till we got to the edge of the cut. There, my horse bumped against a big boulder which sent him up a few feet. It's foolish to mention that I didn't connect with that boulder. I'll just say that I got a glance of it and that somehow I missed it. I was throwed up in the air to the length of my stirrup and there I broke loose from it; but I was no better off it seemed like, for I still had a good fall due me—I was right over the cut.

What happened in the next half a second couldn't be seen for dust and sliding dirt and boulders. I sure had my weather eye out for my horse in that time for I knowed he wasn't far from me, and I didn't want to roll with him no more nor be nowheres near him when I come to the bottom.

The cut, as I found out, wasn't such a bad place to come down into if you was by yourself, but it sure was no place to run into while

I was throwed up in the air to the length of my stirrup and there I broke loose from it.

a-setting on top a head-fighting, runaway bronk. I think I made the bottom of the cut first because I was there to hear something heavy locate amongst the rocks and what little brush growed there. I guess it was about a minute before I started to feel around, not at my ribs but at a sort of choking noise that was near. I couldn't see for the dust that was still soaring, but by sounds I got to reaching out and pretty soon I felt the nostrils and hot breath of my horse. He was upside down and laying quiet, and, if it hadn't been for the choking noise he was making, you'd never knowed he was there.

He was pretty well winded and about through for a spell. I fell on his head to hold him down while I investigated, and I found that most of his body was resting on his neck. So seeing that he couldn't get away from me for a spell, I held out for a few seconds a-trying to gather up some wind for myself. Besides, I figgered this would be a daggone good lesson for that horse, leaving him lie there that way; the next time he might be more careful as to how he behaved.

But I couldn't leave him lie that way long or he'd soon been done for. The dust had cleared a little, then I seen that, being the horse was laying on a slope, it'd be easy for me to help. He could of got up out of there himself only the wind had been knocked out of him so bad that he couldn't even wiggle an ear; without a little help he'd sure died there within a few minutes.

The company I was working for at the time thought more of their horses than they did their cowboys. A dead cowboy was no cash loss to them but a horse was, but I didn't think of that nor of my bruises as I started straightening out that pony; to me he was a horse. I didn't care if he did belong to the company, and besides it was a long ways back to camp. I reached up, grabbed a hold of his tail and pulled down the hill for all I was worth. He soon begin to squirm and as he got a little air it wasn't long till he begin to help. Then, finally, I managed to slide his body down some more and off his neck. At last his head came up to the clear but it sure was a dazed looking head and them nostrils of his was sure wide open for air.

He layed there on all fours for a spell, and, a-holding on of the hackamore rope, I begin to look over the wreck, and a wreck it sure was. It looked like the pony's ears was shoved right down his head, that head was all scarred up, the foretop and the mane was matted with cockle burrs and twigs and weeds, his whole body was covered with dirt; and then I got a glimpse of my saddle. That glimpse showed me that here was a hundred and thirty-five dollars all shot to pieces: the horn was mashed flat into the fork, the leather was scraped off the seat and the cantle was layed low and flapping, the fine carving on the skirts and stirrup leathers was full of long, jagged gashes. Over two months' wages gone in less than ten minutes and on a thirty-five dollar bronk.

I've had a few saddles tore up before and since but never half as bad as this one was, but that all is in the day's riding and I felt mighty lucky, after I got to thinking it over, that it was the saddle and not me that done the connecting with the boulder and stumps. For, as it was, outside of some skin missing here and there, a few bruises, and part of my shirt gone, I was just about the same and still able to earn my wages.

The horse hadn't got by so well and I had to give him a good ten minutes to recuperate in. He'd got up on his feet, looked around, shook himself and soon as he snorted at me again is when I figgered he was okay.

But he was pretty tame on the way into camp, and when a couple of bunches of cattle was throwed my way to turn down toward the main drive (we was on round up) I put him to work just the same.

The next time I rode that horse, about a week or so later, he was just as fit as ever; if anything, he was more fit than ever because he never offered to stampede with me again. I think he figgered I had something to do with the way he bounced on the big boulder and fell into the cut. Then again, me being around when he first come to down there might of had some more to do with it. Maybe he thought I was a bad hombre to fool with.

But he didn't have any of the best of me because I sure didn't think he should mix with angels, and now,—whenever I glance at that little piece of twisted pine limb that caught in my stirrup and remember how I got it, (it had stuck to the stirrup through the whole commotion and I had to pry it loose) I sure am glad that my stampeding and bucking ponies are all on paper and canvas.

"One That Won"

I've often said, even before I had sense enough to care much, that I'd rather ride a raw bronk, fresh from the wild bunch, than a horse which had been monkeyed with for months, and then turned bad.

With a raw bronk, or unbroke horse, that's just run in off the range, there's one thing which a rider can bank on without a doubt, and that is that he's not wise to the human and his ways. He's plum green, and he'll fight only to get away. Where with a horse that's been monkeyed with for months, and then turned bad, you've got something that's not green no more. He'll know how to fight, and when. Them kind of horses will know just the minute something goes wrong, and they'll sure do everything but behave while a rider is in a fix. Then's the time when they bring in their dirty work and add on all the extra licks they can.

Like one time I was coming in from a long ride on a horse which I figgered was a little spoilt. He'd been caught, rode a few times, and then turned loose, caught again, rode a few times more, and turned loose a second time, and a third time, and so on till that pony's main ambition got to be on being turned loose and nothing else.

He got so he'd frame it up so that would happen oftener, and he didn't care what he done to a rider just so he could be turned loose that way. He had many tricks, his main one being to catch a rider asleep, as we call it, or not watching while riding him. He'd just buck him off then if he could and make himself hard to catch.

The longest rest he had was when he crippled a man, because then, being there was only one rider at that camp, he'd be turned loose and wouldn't be rode again till his victim mended or till another rider came along. He'd had pretty good luck that way, and when everything failed sometimes, he'd even play that he was lame. That brought the same results, and no matter which leg he used each time, he'd be turned loose.

Nobody told me of that pony's record when I went to work for that outfit and drawed him in my string; it's not the custom on any outfit anyway, because a cowboy is expected to know what to watch out from any horse the minute he dabs his rope on him, which he does sure enough.

So, that pony didn't catch me asleep when he snorted a greeting at me the first time I caught him. He opened up his bag of tricks and

He had many tricks, one being to catch a rider asleep. He'd buck him off then if he could.

I got to know 'em pretty well, all excepting that stunt of his which was to play lame. I fell for that and turned him loose for two weeks.

It was my second or third ride on him after that two weeks rest when this little story I want to tell of happened.

I was riding back to camp after a good day's work on that horse. I'd been moving beef cattle out of one big pasture into another, and I figgered the horse was pretty tired because it'd been a lot of work and besides he acted that way; but that was just one of his little tricks, to catch me napping, as I found out later. I ought to knowed that too, but I was a little tired myself and maybe I'd got a little careless.

I'd got off to open a long wire gate, and as I led him thru it there didn't seem to be a snort left in him. He just looked tired and caring for nothing much only to get back to camp.

Then, as I went to get on him again, I noticed that my saddle was pretty loose. It wasn't a good idea to have a loose saddle on that horse no time, he might slip right out of it—so, being he acted so tame like, I wasn't so careful as I might of been as I came close to him.

But I was close to his shoulder where I belonged when I reached for the latigo to draw it up. The latigo having been wet with sweat a while back and now being stiff and dry wouldn't slip thru the cinch ring. I had to yank at it, and when I did was when something happened.

I of a sudden felt a hoof connecting with my right leg and close to the hip, and the blow spun me around like I'd been on a pivot. My leg felt numb and useless all at once, and to make things worse that horse tried to jerk away from me.

It was only thru second nature that I hung on to one bridle rein as I was sent up a whirling, the same as a sailor might hang on to a boat in a rough sea; for out on the big range a horse means as much to a cowboy as a boat does to a sailor when no land is near. A long stretch of ground is just as liable to get you when you lose your horse as a long stretch of water would when you lose your boat.

So, natural like, I hung on to that one rein for all I was worth, but it kept a slipping as my horse spun me around like a top and tried to jerk away, and I figger now that no sailor ever had as rough a boat to hang onto as I did then.

Finally, as my hand slid along the rein, it come acrost a knot. It was the end of the rein, and I'd kept a knot tied there just for such happenings as this so I'd know how much slack I could give and still have something to hang onto that wouldn't slip.

When my hand felt that knot during the commotion it would of took a crowbar to pried it loose. But I didn't think I had much chance to hold that horse then, because one leg and hip being useless I couldn't manoeuvre around to get a footing, and the best I could do was to hang on and drag.

And that I was doing in fine shape, because that pony was hitting for the tall and uncut. He was at the height of his glory now, and proceeded to try and scatter me all over the flat. I was drug thru sage and buck brush, alkali and rocks, and pretty often I seen the shadow of a far-reaching hoof come acrost my face. He was trying to kick me loose.

But I hung on. My shirt was tore off by pieces and some skin with it, all the way from my face to my waist. From my waist down I was protected with good old shap' leather. My hurt leg didn't bother me much then because I didn't have time to think about it, but I know it sure didn't help me any. I'd got to thinking that pony would never get tired of dragging me when pretty soon the earth begin to slow up under me and the brush didn't claw quite so hard. Then, and just as sudden as he'd started, the horse stopped, turned, and the length of the rein away, he faced me and snorted. I'd been too much of a drag for him to keep on going with.

It seemed like I laid still for five minutes after he stopped. For one thing I wanted him to cool down some, and I didn't want to jump up and scare him some more. That'd be another good excuse for him to start all over. And then again I wanted to sort of tally up on myself to see what part of me was still in working order.

Still hanging on to the bridle rein, I finally begin to squirm a little. The horse snorted at the first move I made, and then I noticed that my leg wasn't so numb no more. Instead of that I got to feeling a lot of pain, and I found I could hardly move it. A ligament or something was tore sure, I thought, or maybe a bone was broke—it felt like it.

I was in a fine fix— Here I was, a good ten miles from camp, and worse than afoot, because it took a man with two good legs and everything else good to get on that horse, any time. I couldn't ride, and I couldn't stay there.

But as they say, where there's a will there's a way. In my case tho it was more "when you *have to* you can" and so on. Anyway, after I got to figgering things out a spell I made up my mind to *ride*, and being I had no choice I was going to ride that horse.

The hardest part for me to figger out was how to get on him, because with one leg dragging I sure was in no shape to get in the saddle like I should. He'd just take advantage of me if I tried that and maul me around some more. It was then that I, natural like, thought of my rope. A cowboy can do a whole lot with them things when he's in a pinch.

I eased myself up on my good leg, made an awful face as I tried to balance myself there, and then begin to hop towards the horse. But every hop I made towards him scared him, and he kept a backing away out of my reach. Seeing that wouldn't work I tried then to put a little weight on my bum leg so I wouldn't have to hop so much, and even tho that brought me a lot of pain I managed to do that some, and inch by inch I begin to get closer.

The horse kept a watching me like a hawk and cocked an ear at me as I got closer and closer to his shoulder. I sure hoped he didn't blow up then because I'd had no chance to get away. I worked my left hand up and down in easy motion till I touched his neck and kept a working till I got hold of the cheek of the bridle. That done, I rested a spell because the pain in my leg was making me weak.

After a while I went on again, with my right hand this time, and started rubbing along his neck till I got to the withers. Then I slowly reached over and begin to unbuckle the strap that held my rope. The horse begin to snort and act up a little when he seen the rope move, but I was lucky enough to get it, and not any too soon, for the next second he'd snorted away from me and went to the end of the rein again.

I had to start all over in getting up to him, and queer I thought how he realized I was handicapped, because I'd never had much trouble getting up to him before; he wasn't so bad only to get onto. Anyway, I felt better now. I had my rope in my hand and soon I'd have him pegged down where I could whisper in his ear without any back talk from him.

First tho, and before I started flashing a rope around him, I figured I better fix that horse so he wouldn't try to jerk away from me again. He was acting like he might most any second, and I sure didn't want to have him drag me thru any more sage-brush.

I dropped the loop end of my rope with most of the coils to the ground and took the other end, and slow, on account of the pain every move brought, I eased towards the horse's head once more. He kept a backing away from me as before, but after a while I got to touch him on the neck again. Then, not losing any time, I slipped the end of the rope thru the left ring of the bridle bit, and drawed on it till it reached the rigging ring of the saddle, and there I tied it to stay.

I drawed a long breath after that was done because I felt then that I had my horse, and he wouldn't drag Willie over the flat any more. The contraption I'd put on him was what we call a draw rein. I could now turn his head with my little finger, and with all the coils of rope I had left on the ground I had plenty to hang on with.

But I wasn't thru with him yet. I took the loop end of my rope, and now, hopping on one leg all I pleased, I made a loop, and while the horse snorted and pawed the air I begin to aim that loop at his front feet. I was handicapped so that I spilled quite a few throws before I got them front feet of his, but when I did I sure done a good job, because I got both of 'em in a figure eight.

That was no more than done when Mr. Horse quit his fighting right now. He knowed what a rope around his front feet would do to him if he didn't behave, so he stood still and behaved; and I felt like patting myself on the back for the contraption I'd invented out of one rope which started from the rigging ring thru the bridle and down to his front feet. I had the middle of the rope in my hands, and even tho I could just hop around like an old man, I had that ornery horse where I could do anything I wished with him. He was wise enough to know it too.

The next question was to get in the saddle. That was going to be a hard one even if I could get the horse to stand still, but it was my intentions to ride, so at it I went.

I looked around my waist for a piece of my shirt. I wanted to use that for a blindfold and cover up that pony's bad eye which he kept on me so steady. His hind feet was still free and I knowed from my experience a short while before that he'd sure use 'em if he seen his chance. I knowed how far ahead he could reach with 'em too.

But as luck would have it I found enough of the remains of my shirt to cover his eyes with, and that I was very careful in doing. His goose was cooked now more than ever because he didn't know where I was nor what I was doing.

I reached down then and unfastened the rope off his front feet, but I done that in such a way that he'd think the rope was still

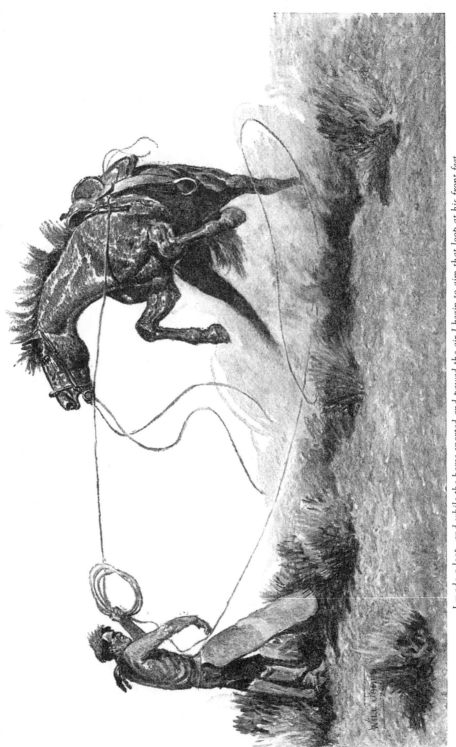

I made a loop, and while the horse snorted and pawed the air I begin to aim that loop at his front feet.

holding, for I only left it wrapped around so I could pull it up and free him after I got in the saddle.

Lucky, I thought as I prepared to climb on, that it was my right leg that was on the blink instead of my left, because with my left I could get up on the side which I was used to, and the horse would be more apt to stand. I grabbed a hold of some mane with one hand and the saddle horn with the other and put most of my weight on my arms. The horse kind of trembled all over and snorted as he felt my weight but he never budged, he was afraid to; then I eased my left foot in the stirrup, slowly raised myself up and leaned well over the fork of the saddle, and taking my right hand off the saddle horn I reached for the bum leg and brought it over the cantle to rest on the right side of the horse.

If that horse had made a move while I was doing that I think I'd just fell off because the pain was a plenty as it was; but luck was with me, and weak with the hurt I finally managed to straighten up in the middle of the saddle where I belonged.

The next thing now was to get this horse to going towards camp without him bogging his head and try to buck me off. I knowed this was the kind of a chance he'd always looked for and he'd sure take advantage of it soon as he felt he was foot loose, but I was aching for anything but jolts right then, and if he did act up with me it sure wouldn't be because I let him.

With the blindfold still over his eyes I drawed the rope up from around his feet, coiled it and tied it to the saddle. The other end of the rope was still thru the bit as a draw rein, and I used the leverage I had on that to bring his head around and, as we say, set it right in my lap.

I took the blindfold off then, and kept it for future use on the way to camp, for I figgered I'd need it some more before I got there.

The horse was free. I gave him his head, and he snorted as he lifted one foot and the other, mighty careful like, to make sure no rope was there to trip him, and then, seeing he was sure enough foot loose, he went on to do just what I thought he would. He started to bogging his head with intentions to try and buck me off right there and then, but he hadn't as yet been made acquainted with that draw rein I still had on his head, and when, without much effort, I brought it up so his nose touched my knee was when that pony got the surprise of his life.

The most he could do was crowhop around a little, and that not being at all encouraging for him, he soon stopped it. But it wasn't any too soon for me. I yanked on the draw rein till all orneriness went out of his head for that time, whirled him around a few times till him and me both got dizzy, and then lined him out for camp at a fast walk.

It was pitch dark by then, and I can't say that I enjoyed that ride on in. What with the pain every step he made brought me, and then watching for every bad move he'd make, and catching 'em in time, so he wouldn't get the best of me, and all, sure didn't leave much for me to grin at before I reached camp.

Then again, I run acrost two gates to open and close before I got there. I had to get off at both of them gates because they wasn't the kind that could be opened or closed from the back of such a horse as I was riding. I spent near an hour getting off and on my horse at each gate, because each time I had to put the blindfold over the horse's eyes, throw the loop end of my rope around his front feet, and get him to stand. It was all near the same as what I've already described only the horse didn't get to drag me around like he did the time he kicked me. But I had to grit my teeth at every move I made, and when I finally got to camp I didn't get there any too soon because the way my whole right leg and hip was hurting I don't think I could of brought myself to make another move.

So, whether it was luck on his part, or scheming, that horse managed to get three long weeks rest from that day's happening. It took me that long to recuperate so I could be able to ride him again; and from that dealing with him, and others of his kind, is where I finally got to prefer a raw uneducated bronk, fresh from the wild bunch, rather than one that's been handled and turned loose and spoiled.

A raw bronk would of snorted a warning as I reached for the latigo to cinch up the saddle; his fighting would of been in the open, where with this man-wise horse he played possum and acted tired so I wouldn't be watching him too close and so he could slam me one to the best advantage.

But I didn't hold it against that horse for what he done to me—no rider who hires out to ride that kind of horse ever does—and if a cowboy gets laid up after a mix-up with one of them ponies he most usually blames himself for letting the horse get the best of him.

I figgered I'd been slipped up on because I wasn't watching close enough. He'd put one over on me, and as I watched him graze in the big pasture while recuperating I felt like he was the winner and I was just the loser.—From watching his chance, catching me when I wasn't looking, and placing a kick at the right time, he'd won out on his main ambitions which was on being turned loose and nothing else. The happening was just another feather in his foretop.

WILLJAMES
—30

V

ON THE DRIFT

"It must be great to be a cowboy, so free and have nothing to do but ride and ride and ride."

That's what a feller says to me one time. I didn't answer him, just sort of grinned at him and says "You bet." . . . There'd been only one way of answering him, not with words, but with a chance for him to try and be a cowboy for a year or so . . . and then I'd like to heard what he'd have to say.

Of course he might of fooled me and liked it, but I'm thinking that his ideas of the life would of changed a heap.

Like for instance. . . .

We was gathering big beef steers one fall. That was up in the northern prairies and where you could ride thirty miles in any direction without striking a break or hollow that was any deeper than a buffalo wallow. The weather had been acting mighty queer, and as the old timers said, queerer than they'd ever seen it. One morning would be fine and clear and warm, too warm, by noon there'd be a wind spring up and bring on thunder showers, and by sundown we'd be digging up all the clothes we owned and putting 'em on to break the cold wind. By the time night come and when we all had to take turns about on guard there'd be a regular blizzard howling, stinging snow would be hitting our faces and making the beef herd hump up. You'd swear it was middle winter.

We'd be up at four o'clock the next morning. It'd still be snowing and the wind blowing cold, with a dark gray sky hanging over us

"It must be great to be a cowboy, so free and have nothing to do but ride and ride and ride."

like a blanket from the North Pole. We'd put on frozen socks inside of wet boots, most all our clothes would be froze and stiff, so was our saddles and ropes, and every horse in the remuda had a kink in their back, was full of snorts and frisky to handle. The most of 'em bucked, many that hadn't bucked for a long time, and even the gentlest ones was hard to get near after they was caught. The sudden cold sure made 'em mean.

We'd have our coffee and line out to riding before daylight, on a white landscape and facing cold winds under gray skies. By middle forenoon it would stop snowing and then there'd be a break up above, after a while the sun would be showing thru, the clouds would clear away and by noon we'd be back to camp with the morning's round-up and go to shedding most of the clothes we had on. Then it'd turn hot, after a while another wind from another direction would spring up and bring on more thunder showers. Thunder and lightning while there was snow on the ground. And that night it'd be snowing and cold again.

That freak weather lasted for about three days. During that time the round-up wagon had to make camp on the open prairie, many miles from any shelter and wood, and what wood was brought along in an extra wagon was fast dwindling away. The cook was the only one that was allowed to use any of it, no separate fires for us cowboys, we had to use the cook's fire when we could and the twenty of us had a hard time getting a place near it whenever we come into camp.

Our round-up outfit moved camp every day, it took six big horses to pull the chuck wagon acrost the soaked prairie, four to pull the wagon that was loaded with our bed rolls, and four more to pull the wood and water wagon. The tracks of the wagons cut down six inches into the tough sod, and in some places the wheels sunk to the hubs. The country was sure wet, everything was wet, our boots and spurs was all slippery mud, our stirrups was slippery, and so was our horses, slippery to ride.

It would be a few days yet before we'd get thru combing the big prairie for the beef steers that was wanted for the fall shipment, and in that time we'd have to camp where the world was level as a floor, with no extra wood or shelter and where whatever the heavens handed out could sure reach us.

The moisture was fine for the stock, every buffalo wallow was full of water, where water hadn't been the whole summer before and now they was having a chance to get at the tall grass that hadn't been touched during the whole time.

The loose stock was doing fine, and so was the two thousand steers we'd gathered, but with the steers they was getting hard to hold at night, maybe it was from the change of heat during the day to sudden cold and snow during the night. We sure felt that change ourselves and agreed pretty well with the steers that a stampede wouldn't go bad. It'd sort of warm a feller up.

It was on the third night of the stormy weather that the steers did break into a dandy stampede, and even after the wagonboss put four men on each shift and warning us to be sure and hold them steers. I don't think any of us tried to hold 'em any too much, we was cold.

I happened to be on shift when the stampede started, it was during the "grave-yard shift" (from midnight till two), lightning had been playing longer that night, some of it played mighty close to the herd and when one bolt landed to within fifty feet of it and split a big boulder the whole herd just picked itself up like it was one steer and lit out. It wasn't but a minute afterwards when a regular cloud-burst hit us, a feller couldn't see six inches ahead, my horse's feet sunk ankle deep in the sod and in some little swales he'd slip and slide. But he was a good horse and stayed on his feet.

The lightning and rain kept a pattering around us, the herd was running good, but I noticed by the flashes of lightning that it was splitting. I tried to crowd the bunch I had with the main bunch, but in the dark my horse was just another steer and was crowded out of the way and my holler couldn't be heard on account of the noise and

I noticed by the flashes of lightning that the herd was splitting.

splashing. When I got to feeling a few horns alongside of my leg every time I tried to bend my bunch I soon realized that I'd just as well try to turn a locomotive off the track as to try and bend them steers. They couldn't see nor hear me and they was wanting to run.

I tried to bend the leaders time and time again, and kept on trying. I'd hit the closest ones over the head with my coiled rope, but that didn't faze 'em. I emptied my six-shooter in front of their noses, and that checked 'em no longer than the time it took for the flash and report of my shots to die out, then they'd come right on again.

The steers kept on running even after the lightning died down. They was warmed up now, all excited and het up on the subject, and I knowed they'd be hard to stop till they tired out pretty well. That might be five or maybe ten miles from where they'd started.

I kept on doing my best to turn the leaders. We struck prairie dog towns a couple of times and as some steers would stick a leg in a hole and turn over that would check the herd some, but not enough so they wouldn't pick up speed again soon as them towns was crossed, and as the last lightning flashes dimmed away and I tried to locate the main herd by 'em I seen that I was by myself and with a little bunch that'd split loose from it. There wasn't a sign of the main herd or any part of it to be seen nowheres.

I sure missed that lightning because the night was dark as a stack of black cats. The rain kept a pouring, and then a sudden strong wind came up and was so fast that even at the speed I was riding I felt it pushing my horse along. The steers went right with it for a spell, then finally begin to slow down. I had 'em then, and in a few minutes more I got 'em stopped. Stopped, but not turned because none of 'em could be made to face the heavy rain that the wind pounded onto 'em.

I figured I was about seven or eight miles from camp when I got the steers stopped. I knowed I couldn't drive 'em back till the wind and rain let up, for as it was I'd be doing mighty well if I just kept 'em from drifting on. So, there was no chance of being relieved off my shift on guard that night, and I settled down to staying with the cattle and keep 'em from drifting as much as I could.

The heavy rain poured on then it begin to get cold, mighty cold, and I didn't believe it was possible but the wind got stronger, after a while I begin to feel snow on my face and it wasn't long when there wasn't no more rain, it was all snow, real honest-to-god snow, and backed by a real honest-to-god wind. It was one of these blizzards that you sometimes hear about and makes you shiver even while standing by a red hot stove.

To say I was comfortable would sure be a beautiful lie. My slicker was in camp, where most slickers are when you need 'em the most, I had a heavy duck coat on but the rain had went thru that and soon as the cold and snow come it froze stiff. My legs was the only part of me that was dry, they was covered with a good pair of shaps'.

With the blizzard a howling the little herd I had begin to drift. There was no use trying to stop and hold 'em, I'd only wore my horse out and while I'd be riding in front of one part of the herd the other part would keep on drifting anyhow, so I let 'em drift and checked 'em as much as I could by doing as little riding as possible.

I rode in the lead of the herd the rest of the night, and when daylight come and I seen no sign of the blizzard breaking up I didn't try to check the herd no more. It looked now like the storm would be sure to last at least all that day, and knowing that even if some riders did find me and helped that the herd couldn't be turned to face the blizzard I let 'em drift to their hearts' content. They wanted shelter and so did I, and all I done while I shivered and my teeth chattered was to ride around the herd and see that it kept together. It was hard to see them all in the whirling snow but I made a rough count of about a hundred and fifty head, a plenty big enough herd so that no cowboy would leave and let scatter.

I wished now there hadn't been no stampede and that we'd all worked harder to stop it. If it hadn't been for that I'd been in camp now, in the shelter of canvas and drinking hot coffee. As it was it looked like I'd be missing that coffee for sometime to come. I didn't expect any riders out looking for me, if any was it wasn't at all likely they'd find me because in the thick snow a feller couldn't see much further than the length of his horse, and if any riders did find me they couldn't do any more than what I was doing alone, they'd just have to drift too.

I figured that, if I had my directions right, I'd be hitting a creek that I knowed of within fifteen or twenty miles from where I was. The creek cut deep in the prairie had steep breaks on both sides and thick clumps of willows along the banks. There's where there'd be shelter and where the herd would be glad to stop and easy to hold, I could build a fire too as there was plenty of dead wood all along the creek.

The thought of a fire made me do better than to just let the herd drift, I went to driving 'em and making 'em go faster, away from camp and towards that shelter. For the way the weather behaved it looked like it was due to be the same for another day or so, and being I couldn't get back to camp with the herd I hit for shelter, and where I could build a fire.

I went with the wind, kept the herd at a good walk and the steers being all big and strong I made pretty good time. The day wore on that way, the blizzard still a howling right along and in some places the snow had drifted pretty deep. The running, then the drifting and the cold begin to show on the steers, they'd shrunk quite a bit, but being it was early fall with some more warm weather to be expected a few days of good grazing would put 'em back to where they was.

I drove 'em on, expecting any time now to see the leaders drop over the breaks into the creek bottom. I couldn't see the leaders, but it wouldn't be long after they hit the creek when I'd know.

But the creek must of been further than I figured. It was beginning to get dark and I still hadn't got to it, when, as I thought, I should of got to it by the middle of the afternoon. Then I got to wondering, wondering if the wind hadn't switched some and made me loose my direction. As night came on I knowed daggone well that's what had happened, but I didn't think I was far from the creek. I tried to turn the leaders to sidling against the storm, but I had to give that up because none of the leaders nor any in the herd would sidle against the stinging snow and cold wind.

There was nothing for me to do except to let 'em drift with the storm. I knowed for sure by then that we'd missed the creek and I wasn't driving the cattle no more, I just kept 'em together and let 'em drift and settled down to "nothing to do but ride and ride and ride."

Only, sometimes I walked, I had to or I'd of froze stiff. My horse was pretty tired too, and ganted up as much as I was.

It was sure a long night, and I was mighty sleepy, but I didn't dare sleep for fear I'd freeze to death, sleep is the first step to that the rest comes easy. I'd walk till I was tired out then I'd ride till I was about froze and then I'd walk some more. I kept that up all night and drifted on with the herd till finally the sky begin to light up and another day come.

It might be wondered at why I didn't quit the herd and hit back for camp or shelter. There's only one answer to that, it's against cowboy religion and a *cowboy* never quits a herd.

But another day of that blizzard and I would of had to quit the herd, or else my carcass would of been preserved in a snow bank and not been found till the snows melted, maybe away into the following spring. But as good luck would have it, mighty good luck, it wasn't long after daylight come when it quit snowing, the wind had went down a considerable too and now I could see a long ways.

The first thing I noticed was the breaks of the creek I'd been trying to get the cattle to. It was only a couple of miles away and we'd been drifting right along it, most likely all night.

A cowboy never quits a herd.

But now the cattle could be drove back to the main herd at camp, and I sure drove 'em because I figured I had about twenty-five miles to go to get there and I was mighty hungry and sleepy. I was sure glad when a little before noon I seen three riders coming my way, they was from the round-up wagon and out looking for me and my herd, they took charge of the herd an told me to hit for camp. I done that, but before I started I relieved one of the boys from his sack of tabacco, I hadn't had a smoke since early the day before and that was as bad as going without something to eat.

It was while I was rolling a smoke that the boys told me the round-up wagon was moving ten miles down country to meet the herd. The main herd and all had been on the drift. Well, that was ten miles less for me to ride that sure didn't make me mad.

When I found the wagon, the pilot and a few other cowboys was setting up camp, the cook already had the fire going and the coffee was near boiling. I camped right by the fire and that big black pot, drinking cup after cup of the black coffee, and as I begin to warm up some and feeling a little more awake, I got to hearing from the other boys around that I wasn't the only one that had drifted with a split of the herd. For after the stampede had started all hands had got on their night horses to help stop it but they hadn't got there in time to help us who'd been separated each with out little herds. Two other riders had each been left by their lonesome the same as I had.

153

WILL JAMES
30

WILL JAMES
III~26

VI

THE COWBOY CALENDAR

JANUARY

BUCKING THE DRIFTS, AND LOOKING FOR SNOWBOUND STOCK

The winter months in the cow country and to the north take in a lot of bucking one thing and then another. In this case it's snow, but the cold winds that bring them snows is not at all faced without a squint; and the cowboy at his work looking out for weaker stock finds January one of the longest and hardest months of the year.

In this picture it tells some of how the rider is with his horse. The hand on the neck of the pony means "Steady, boy," and the same as to show that both man and horse are *together* in the work.

FEBRUARY

THE END OF A KILLER

*Out from camp a ways the cowboy often
sets his traps and catches Mr. Wolf*

With all the riding there is to do in winters to keep tab
of the stock, break trails for them that's snowbound, cut
drift-fences so the herd might drift on to shelter from the
blizzard that blinds and freezes, then cutting out the weak
ones and starting 'em on the way to the feeding grounds
and where the ranch hands do the work of shoveling good
hay to 'em, and all, there's some more to contend with
and which keeps the cowboy on his horse and moving.
There's the varmints such as coyotes which as a rule begin to fatten up in February on account of the winter
being on for a good spell and which begins to tell on the
weak stock that's sometimes overlooked. The cowboy in
this picture has a few traps set where his day's riding
takes him, and this day he's some lucky, cause instead of
getting the coyote which waits till his victim is down he's
caught a big old gray boy, a wolf. That killer gets his meat
while it's up and strong and fat, but now that bad one
had done come to the end of his trail.

WILL JAMES
11-27

MARCH

THE FIRST BLADES OF GREEN

*The sight of which will sure make a cowboy
glad after the long winters*

There's no country in the world, I don't think, where the first patch of green is as appreciated as it is in the range countries of the Northwest. Maybe I feel that way about that on account of the long winters I've put in there myself. I well remember how it struck me when March would come along, and then on the sunny side of a ridge the snow had melted away leaving a patch of warm earth a-steaming to the sun, and real green grass which throwed a perfume the likes of which could never be bought in bottles. I could seldom help but let out a glad war-whoop at the sight, and slide my horse to a standstill right there. That patch of green, even though it'd again be covered with flurries of wet snow, was there to say that old man Winter was giving away. Soon there'll be no more weak cattle to keep track of, they'll be all picking up fat and strength, and the whole world will be a-smiling again.

APRIL

GATHERING THE REMUDA

The month when the cowboys begin shedding off their heavy coats and often wish before they get back to camp that they'd kept 'em on. The green grass has come up to take the place of the snow, and the result is there's no more weak stock for the cow-man to worry about.

The riders are out gathering the saddle horses, and them ponies having many long months' rest on the pick of the range are not at all easy to catch up to and turn. They're fat, and the long winter hair falling off in big patches leaves a slick shiny hide. As the cowboy hazes the ponies toward the big corrals where the *remuda* is gathered, he rides by many a cow what looks up at his coming but keeps on a-chewing on tall blades of green. The little feller that's by her side looks up too, and all interest, but he don't as yet know what all this horse-chasing is about. He don't know that these running ponies he's seeing will soon be packing riders to round up him and his kind, and being so young he ain't worried none.

MAY

THE SPRING ROUND-UP

If the winter is of average, and spring is not too slow in coming, the spring round-up starts in this month. A wagon goes out loaded with grub and the cowboys' own rolls of bedding. Wherever that wagon is, is where the riders gather when the work is done. It is camp.

Following after the wagon there comes what's called the "remuda," which is a herd of saddle-horses furnished by the company for the riders. The wrangler hazes them along to every camp and sees that the ponies are in the rope corral whenever the riders need fresh horses. The spring round-up is when the new calves all get the markings and brand of the outfit the mother belongs to, and in this picture that's just what's happening.

JUNE

THE HORSE ROUND-UP

Every good-size cow-outfit owns many horses, some of 'em up to thousands. Out of them they get their saddle- and work-horses, and once in a while if the market is good a few carloads is shipped out. It takes many horses to run a cow-outfit. Every rider is furnished from six to twelve head of 'em at one time, and then at the ranches there's a lot of work, and the ranchhands need many work-horses to put up the hay that's needed to carry the cattle through when a hard winter comes.

The horse round-up, as a rule, starts after the cow work is over in the spring. These are what's called stock-horses, taking brood-mares, unbroke geldings, studs and colts. There's no saddle-horses amongst these unless it's some old pony that's been pensioned off and has the privilege of running about the range with whatever he pleases. These horses are being rounded up so that the colts can all be branded and perhaps a few of them cut out and held at the home ranch to be broke.

JULY

RIDING FOR A PRIZE

There's not a lot of work on the range in July, and it's a
kind of a good thing too, on account of the fourth of that
month's celebrations when every cowboy that can is in
town. Rodeos are pulled off here and there, and the range-
riders are the boys that makes them rodeos what they are.

The cowboy in this picture is celebrating for all he's
worth, and at the same time riding for a prize. When the
four-day celebration is over, he'll go back to the range
again, to the line camp, or to the breaking-pens where
he's got a steady job, breaking horses.

AUGUST

SNAPPING BRONCS

Horse-breaking comes pretty near being a year-round job, and you're just as apt to see the bronco-buster at work on a wintry Christmas day as you are any other time; but as a rule, most horses are run in to be broke in the spring and middle summer. Middle summer is the best time in some countries on account that as soon as a bronc is "started," he can be put on the fall works, so he has a chance to learn a lot while there's good feed to keep him in shape.

The cowboy in this picture is "starting" his horse in the way most riders do. That pony's hind foot being tied not only keeps him from kicking at the rider, but it hinders him considerable in his acting up while the saddle is slipped on his back. The rider puts the saddle on with one hand, and with the other on the hackamore rope, he keeps the horse's head where it belongs. A simple twist of the wrist does the trick, if the twist is at the right time.

SEPTEMBER

Line-Riders

The line-riders' job is to see that none of the company's cattle get out of their territory and that none other stray in. Tracks and many signs tell the line-riders all they want to know every day about the location of the cattle, and they don't have to see them to know where they are. Line-riders also keep the cattle-thief pretty well out of the company's range, because with them on the job, the thief's trail, with the cattle, would be found within a few hours. September brings line-riding pretty well to an end, and most of them leave their line camps at that time to join the round-up wagon for the fall works. These two boys in the picture are caught in the act of trying to count the days until they can get with "the spread" again.

OCTOBER

Cutting Out

Beef round-up and shipping time

The fall round-up is on full swing. Herds are gathered; late spring calves are branded, and all that's missed during the spring round-up; then with their mammies they're drove to some corral where the calf is separated from his mother to be weaned. The "weaner" calf, being five or six months old, don't suffer none from the weaning; he's had strong rich milk all summer, all his mammy gave, and along with the grass that he kept filled up on, he's more than husky now.

With the fall branding and weaning there comes the beef-gathering. Fine big steers are brought to the cutting grounds, cut out, put into the main herd and afterwards culled till none but "tops" are left to make up the beef herd.

WILL JAMES
'27

NOVEMBER

The End of the Season

*The cowboys that are not kept on payroll catch up
their private ponies and hit out with the birds*

The fall round-up is over; the beef herd has been drove
to the shipping pens at the railroad and loaded in the stock-
cars; the old stock has been brought close to the feeding
grounds, and the work of the season with the round-up
wagon comes to an end. The *remuda* (saddle-horse bunch)
is being corraled for the last time for the year; some of the
boys are catching their private ponies, which, after a long
summer's grazing and rest, are more than ready to travel
into whatever new territory the cowboy might head 'em
for. With his saddle on one horse and his tarpaulin-covered bed on another, the rider never cares much where
the trail ends—it'll be in some new country with a winter's
job breaking horses, or else holing up in some deserted
cabin from which he'll spread out a line of traps and
make winter wages on coyotes and bobcats.

DECEMBER

The Winter Camp

Christmas is only another day at a cow camp

By the cottonwood-timbered creeks of the cow-country are scattered one-or two-roomed cabins which make up the cow-camps of every outfit. The riders that stay with the outfit the year around are paired off to each camp where they're to ride through the winter and keep an eye on whatever stock which will need feeding; one or two "hay-shovelers" (ranch hands) are there to feed whatever stock the riders bring in. Sometimes there's a cook to help along in such camps, and as the winter sets in and the coulees fill up with drifts, the work accumulates till all hands are kept mighty busy. And the work goes on the same if the sun is shining or a blizzard is howling. Christmas comes as just another day, and as the year dies out and the town folks are celebrating the coming of the new year, the rider is apt to be in some draw figgering ways to get around snowbanks with some little bunch of weak stock he's bringing in to camp.

VII

THE RODEO

From the Ground Up

Mighty few people in the grandstands at a Rodeo have a chance to know or learn what the goings-on down below 'em in the big arena is all about. Most all go wild at watching the contest between man and animal and man and man, but they look at that the same way as I look at a football game and even tho I appreciate a lot of the goings-on with the players in the football game my interest is cut to half on account I don't understand it.

In this story I'd like to have you see the Rodeo from the ground up and take you along with me into the arena and have you meet some of the cowboys and cowgirls that's contesting. Have you see some of our bucking horses and wall-eyed longhorn steers, and notice how the horses and steers look bigger down here and seem a lot wilder. I want you to get the feel of 'em for what they are and I'll see that you're in a safe place when the chute gate opens and a bucking horse or wild steer comes out. While you're watching the bucking animal *from the ground* and feeling the earth shake under you you'll be listening to the cowboy's talks and learn their pedigrees.

But before I take you down in the Arena I want to tell you a bit of how the Rodeo come to be. . . . The word Rodeo is Spanish for round-up and is pronounced Ro-day-o. The meaning of Rodeo or round-up on the range is where cattle are brought in from the hills and plains and put into one herd by the riders, that's everyday happening and a heap of that is done yet these days. The Rodeo such as you see in Madison Square Garden, Cheyenne, Pendleton, Calgary, Salinas, Tucson, Fort Worth and many a place started near fifty years ago. The California Spanish with their million acre grants put on the first ones, but in a little different style and that was about two hundred years ago, they lasted for days and when hearing of some Don putting on a fiesta, real barbecue with wine and doings, there was a sure enough gathering, or Rodeo, of many vaqueros (cowboys) on the job to take on the fun and the sports of them days. They must of had a lot of fun and, as an old Spaniard told me some years ago they had a lot of sports too. The main sport and contest was roping, and them Spaniards was sure wizards with the rope. I know because I rode with many that come from the same breed. They could take that seventy-foot string of braided rawhide, sail it out and it seemed alive in their hands and they had as much control with the end that was far away as the one that was in the hand.

The contest that was watched the most was where two vaqueros would be using them snaky coils at one another. There'd be a champion roper and a challenger, or better yet, there'd be two vaqueros fighting a duel that way. It was with the same spirit as I figure two gladiators would go for one another but not near as awkward-like. (As for me, if I couldn't of seen my way clear of a get away I'm sure I'd of took the lance and armor instead of the rawhide rope to fight a duel with.) Anyway, the two vaqueros would ride to within twenty feet or so of one another and make passes back and forth with the loops. The idea was for each one to spoil the other's throw with his own loop and, sparring that way, watch for an opening. When there was an opening and the loop of the oponent was an inch in the clear the other feller would slip his past like a shot and, if he caught that oponent, which was a cinch he would, well it'd be just all off for him. If that oponent was just in a contest he'd be jerked off his horse and drug around only a little ways, but if it was during a duel the feller that was unlucky enough to get snared would be drug away and the winner wouldn't be riding back till only a shank of hair was left in his loop.

That was about the only rough doings they had at them first Rodeos, excepting maybe a little bull fighting such as they have in Spain but, as some old Spaniards told me who seen the last of such doings, they sure had a lot of fun. One of the old Spaniards who I still remember well on account I was riding on the same outfit he was, he was still riding for a living when past ninety years old and still one of the best ropers in the country. That was in Nevada and near twenty years ago. There was ladies for the higher-up vaquero to dance with, he said, a steady run of good music and the Don seen to it that the Indians kept the wine jars full and the barbecue pits with hot coals and plenty of meat along 'em to carve from.

The first contest I ever seen which could, in a way be classed with the Rodeos of to day was up on the line of Montana and Canada. It was a gathering of about twenty thousand head of cattle, there was near a hundred cowboys to handle 'em. The cattle was in five different herds, one herd had just been trailed from a ways South and going further North, another that changed ownership and was to be throwed into another herd, there was one that was just changing range and another that was made up mostly of strays which had drifted South the winter before. All them herds and the cowboys that handled 'em happened to come together along the trail and waiting for inspection before crossing the line into Canada.

Well, in that bunch of cowboys there was a kind of gathering from near every state where there is cowboys, from Texas, New Mexico and Arizona on North, many of 'em had different ways of roping and riding, and, as the herds was being held and rested for a couple of days there got to be some betting from different camps as to which one could do this or that better than the other. On the last

day the betting got so that something had to be done and the foremen had to give in and let the boys have some stock to show their
skill with. Best roping horses was produced, and fast longhorns.
The South won on the roping, easy, but when the big snorty northern horses was produced for the bucking contest the northern riders sure won the money there.

I was a whole lot of a kid when I set on my horse and watched
that contest but I'll sure never forget the sight, with prairie sod for
an Arena, thousands of cattle around, round-up wagons, hundreds
of saddle horses and all that spells cowboy without using a letter. I
think I'd give my right ear and part of my left to see that again.

As I've already said, Rodeo or round-up means gathering, and an
old cowboy tells me that the first gathering where there was no big
herd of cattle and cowboys only formed the gathering was at Cheyenne, Wyoming. The round-up of cowboys came there from all
around and to contest for the championship of steer roping and
bronk riding. That was one of the first contests where there was to
be prizes offered for such and where there'd be a crowd buying
tickets and setting around to witness the doings.

That was close to forty years ago, and before I'd let out my first
squawk or I'd sure been there.

I was about sixteen when I first heard of a Rodeo, and when I
found out what it was, that it was where cowboys could win a prize
for riding or roping I caught my own horse, quit the whole outfit
flat and hit the sixty miles for where the Rodeo was to be pulled off.
I had a lot of confidence in my riding ability by then, I hadn't been
bucked off for the last six months and got to be a pretty good rider,
I thought, forgetting the hundred times I'd been bucked off before.

The Rodeo and gathering was to be pulled off in the main street
of the town and was to last one whole afternoon. I entered for
bucking horse riding (it's called bronk riding now) and drawed my

horse's name out of a hat where the names of all the bucking horses was wrote down on little folded pieces of paper.

My first horse must of took pity on me because every time he'd send me up where there was no chance of me coming back in the saddle only by a miracle he'd produce the miracle and come right under where I was a hanging on thin air. Well, I passed, or qualified on that first horse.

But the second one I drawed didn't take as good a care of me and on about the fifth jump I looked down to see my shadow on the ground instead of a horse and soon my shadow came up and met me.

Well, I'd entered in a couple other events such as roping and the wild mule race and after getting all skinned up I finally came out the winner of ten whole dollars, after spending a hundred dollars and losing three days work. I sure had a lot of fun tho, and on the fourth day I rode the sixty miles back to the outfit.

It wasn't many years after that when Rodeos got to be more and more heard of, even if they was pulled off a thousand miles away and the cow camps was a hundred miles from the railroads we'd somehow get word of the doings, and the prizes getting bigger and bigger every year made many a cowboy hit out from his home range for a spell and try his luck on the picked bucking horses, or at making fast time in steer roping and bulldogging.

There was many new events brought in the Rodeos by then which had been figured on for years and which us boys had never heard of, also the rules and regulations had been making it harder for a cowboy to qualify. Every contest had new and different rules but even as hard as them got to be they was easy as compared to what they are to day. To day the cowboy that reaches the finals and wins first in any event sure has to go some to win in that event, the animal has got a whole lot the advantage of the cowboy.

Let's go into the Arena now and to the corrals where the stock is, let's see the bucking horses first. We come to where bales of hay are stacked to feed the stock and amongst the bales are cowboys laying here and there, some catching up on sleep they didn't get the night before and resting a bit before the contest starts, others are laying and sort of groaning while broken bones are mending. They should go to the hospital you might say, well, most of 'em did first but soon came out packing their splints and casts, them that didn't come out was because they couldn't. A cowboy would take a jail any time before he would a hospital. . . . Some of the cowboys all skinned up and groaning there will be in the contest again this afternoon and bull-dogging and bronk riding. They got to or lose out, and it's a long ways back home.

I seen many a cowboy ride a bronk with a broken ankle or bull-dog a steer with a dislocated shoulder.

You might wonder if the Rodeo management stands the doctor's expense in case a contestant gets hurt and, as to that it says on prize and rule lists of every Rodeo that the contestant contests at his or her own risk "and each participant by the act of entry or participation waives all claim against the management for any injuries they or their stock may sustain."

Well, here's the bucking horses, doing nothing but eating a lot of good hay. They don't look so wild right now, just to look at 'em. They're about the size of what's called a big hunter in the East.

I've often been asked if them horses ain't trained to buck, and to that I have to smile when I say, "Well, they ain't been discouraged from it, but to train 'em to buck would be like trying to train an eagle how to fly."

These bucking horses are all western range horses, they run free and wild like antelope and many are not run in or get a rope on 'em till they are eight or ten years old. The buckers are the picked worse

183

To train them horses to buck would be like trying to train an eagle how to fly.

ones of a bad bunch of outlaws. Johnnie Mullens, Eddie Mc-Carty, Johnson, Leo Cramer and such men as them who contract with the Rodeos to furnish bucking stock and travel the whole West over looking out for good bad horses. They may not go any distance to pick up a good saddle horse but they'll sure ramble when they hear some cowboy tell of a wampus-cat bucking horse.

Every western horse has got the buck in him. Some never show it but it's there and it'll come out if something sticks him at the wrong place when he ain't looking. One of the best bucking horses I ever seen had never made a jump till he'd been rode for four years. He was gentle as a kitten and a fine cowhorse, then something went wrong one day and he bucked his man off. After that he turned out to be a regular wolf and he was finally sold and throwed in the bucking string.

No, we don't have to train horses to buck. If anything we try to keep 'em from it but if they're inclined to do nothing else but that they're no good to do any range work with and if they can buck hard enough you'll see 'em doing it at their heart's content in the middle of an Arena.

Many people have asked me if the strap that goes around a horse's flanks ain't what makes him buck, some even think there's tacks in it. The horse would buck as good without the strap but the strap makes him buck a little different and acts only as a sort of a reminder around his ticklish flanks, something like slipping an icicle down somebody's back. The rider suffers more from that strap than the horse does, he's the one who has to take the jolts.

Here comes riders now who's took many such jolts. They're fellers who the last few years won championships in such contests as Calgary, Pendleton, Cheyenne and New York where the biggest of such doings is pulled.

"Hello, Jack (This is Jack Shields who once won in Calgary) when did you hit town, and how?"

And here comes Turk Greenough and Paddy Ryan. Two winners, different years at Pendleton, then along with 'em is Dick Shelton, Earl Thoede, Bob Askins, Howard Tegland and some others.

"Thought the sheriff told you to keep out of town, Bill," one says.

Many grinning remarks come my way, and once in a while I have to dodge a tackle. The boys are headed to get saddle horses for the Grand Entree and I go along. Johnnie Mullens brings me a high stepping horse with a fancy silver mounted saddle on him. "Get on, Bill," and I get on.

I don't care to ride in Grand Entree, and neither do any of the cowboys, too much show stuff, but the committee has a rule that says "all contestants must ride in the Grand Entree."

I'm not a contestant no more, but seeing that fancy saddle I thinks I'll try it, because I'd never rode a silver mounted saddle before. We line up in pairs, cowboys and cowgirls, but there's not near enough cowgirls to go around so, after making one circle of the Arena while the band played loud we get in single file and cut different figures, then after a spell of that we follow the flag back out of the Arena.

Bronk riding is the first event, and the riders that are to be called right away are back to the chutes. One of 'em, Leo Murry, climbs the wide chute gate and eases himself down it into the saddle that's cinched tight on a wall-eyed black outlaw horse called Funeral. . . . It's a dangerous thing to slip both legs around such a horse and get your stirrups, there's just a few inches between him and the heavy chute timbers and if the horse goes to fighting in there, as he most always does, a rider's leg can easy get skinned up and sometimes broke. Some horses will also do their best to reach around and fasten their teeth on a leg too. That can't be seen from the grandstand.

The three judges in the Arena, and with their little books in their hands are ready to mark points for or against the rider. The judges have to judge both the horse and the rider. They got to watch if the horse is bucking good and if the rider is riding good at the same time and mark down the points according. A good rider will lose points on a poor bucking horse, and that's just his bad luck unless the judges allow him a reride on another and better bucking horse.

Well, here comes Funeral. The chute gate is no more than opened when he's out in the Arena, he makes three nice easy jumps and then bows his neck and settles down to bucking. He does that gradual and that's the kind a cowboy likes because it gives him a chance to get to sitting good before the hard bucking comes.

The hard bucking does come but the cowboy rides plum past the judges and according to the rules till the whistle blows.

The next horse that comes out starts bucking right in the chute first and hugs along the chutes afterwards. He sure is crooked and hard hitting and I can feel the cantle of that saddle right thru the ground to where I'm sitting. I glances at Paddy and Bob who's by me, they're not saying a word and neither am I but I can see by the look on their faces that they figured the last ride to be mighty good and all they think of now is if they can do as good or better when they're called to ride.

"What horse did you draw for to day, Bob?"

"Soapy Smith, ain't never seen him rode yet and I don't know how good he is."

"Just my luck to draw 'Ibedamn,'" says Paddy, "he ain't much good no more and with two southern judges out of three it looks like this contest is going to be kind of cold for us northern boys."

Another good bucking horse out with another good rider a-reefing on top of him. He makes a fine ride and the crowd cheers and hollers, but the cowboy never hears a crowd because he's all for watching what the riders he's come to contest with are doing, and sort of balancing his chances all around. Each one knows that he's got to do better than the other in order to win any of the money prizes, "it's a case of no catchum no eat" says a cowboy one time, and so the contestant don't get to appreciate the good work another contestant might do. The crowd appreciates that a heap more even if they do understand a heap less, the crowd comes there for entertainment and the cowboy comes to gather all he can of that stuff that jingles and which buys grub and things.

The only contestant that enjoys the other feller's good work is the one who is contesting in other events than that other feller. A champion roper will be tickled to see a good rider do good work on a tough bronk but he'll be sort of worried when his event comes around and sees some contestant make fast time in roping and tying.

It's the same way in any game and with all of us, when we got to earn a living. And I figure that the cowboy has fell into the hardest, most dangerous and least paying way of making a living, either while following contests or when he's at home on the range.

While he's following contests he's got to raise his own fare and expense money to wherever the contest may be, and if he's wise or else sure of winning some prizes he'll raise enough to come back on too. It takes a lot of money to come from all points West to New York or Chicago, from Texas to Pendleton or Calgary, or from Calgary and Cheyenne to Fort Worth or Tucson. And that ain't all the expense, besides that the cowboy has to pay entrance fees which will cost him on an average of $150, all depends how many events he enters in. One contest last year cost a cowboy $350 to enter in only seven events.

There's four events where the contestants even have to furnish their own horses and outfits. That's in trick and fancy roping, trick riding, calf roping and bull-dogging. The horses that's used in them events sure can't be found everywhere, and so the contestants take their private horses along with 'em at every Rodeo they go to, either in trailers, back of an automobile or by rail. A contestant and his horse will sometime cover ten thousand miles in a few months while getting from one Rodeo to another. That expense is all out of his own pocket, and he's got to be a bear of a hand to make that back, also his entry fees.

Once a cowboy puts his money down so as to enter in different events he never sees that money no more. The management keeps that for good, and what's more, if the cowboy don't act exactly according to rules he's not only apt to be let out of the contest and without chances of winning anything but the money he paid out to enter with is not returned to him.

And that ain't all. There's many little Rodeos who take the cowboys' entrance fees, have 'em contest for three straight days with promises of big prizes, and when comes the time for the prize money to be turned over to the riders there's nothing but excuses handed out, and no money. The cowboys can't do nothing about it, excepting maybe tear up the Rodeo office.

But a Rodeo Association is doing things to check that kind of work, and that association is going to do a heap of other things for it looks to me like Rodeos are goings-on where cowboys and cowgirls throw in their money to pay for their own prizes and trophies, and the gate receipts go to the management. I never heard of any other game where you have to pay to contest. In a prize fight the feller that gets licked often gets a third of the purse but the cowboy that gets throwed off bucking horse and smashed only gets disqualified and let out of the contest. Fares and expenses are paid to football and baseball players and with many other games, and that sure strikes me as it should be.

It should be that way for the cowboy too. He's showing the folks a game of skill and daring that can't be played by anyone but the ones that's *raised* at it. It's something that's learned in Nature's schools and which was handed down from the pioneers who was the first to blaze the trails in the Western plains and mountains.

Amongst the thousand or more contestants that scatter to different Rodeos thruout the U.S.A. there's only about a third that break even and make their own expenses, a fourth will clear enough to take 'em to the next Rodeo, a fifth of 'em will have some money to spare and only one tenth, the top hands and wise to the game will come out with a stake. And such cowboys sure have to rope and ride and bull-dog to make that stake and be mighty lucky at every event that they don't break their necks.

The average bronc rider seldom lasts over eight or ten years at the game, by that time he's pretty well broke up, and he'll either stay on his ranch or take on tamer events. The younger fellers that keep coming in and are steady climbing will then take his place and the game goes on. I don't know of any contestant that ever retired with anything much but a heap of experience, most of the money goes for expenses between Rodeos and getting to the next one. It's a great game for a young feller who has a lot of guts and has learned to ride and rope before he's ten years old.

Once in a while some Rodeo committee will spread itself a bit and offers a silver cup as a trophy to the winner, with some of them cups there is a strong string tied to 'em and the winner has to win the championship three years in succession at that same Rodeo, other championships didn't count. Well, when the cowboy who wins such a cup he feels like he's sure earned it three times and it don't mean much to him, he sometimes gives it to some sweetheart and then forgets the sweetheart and the cup too. If the cup was just plain tin and full of the metal that buys meat and potatoes that would be of more use.

But the cowboy has nothing to say as to that and he's got to go some to win anything. All is mighty uncertain too. . . . Nowata Slim from Oklahoma came to the Chicago Rodeo one year. He was high man in bronk riding and his chances was everything for the championship and nothing else, but, as he just about had the money in his pocket, one little horse called Broken Box and weighing around twelve hundred pounds went out from under him and kicked him in the head before he landed. Consequences was that Nowata didn't only lose the championship prize but he got paralyzed all the way down one side. I went to see Slim at the hotel, he didn't know me nor nobody else nor nothing. . . .

The day before he was strutting around the chutes like he had the world by the tail with a downhill push, and he had, till that fraction of a second when he not only lost the championship but was layed low to boot. . . .

Rose Hartwig, a good, game bronk riding cowgirl was talking to a few of us and says, as she climbed the chute and eased into the saddle how she felt it was to be her "last ride." She came out of the chute on a pretty tough horse, made a good ride and was up for the final money too when, before the pick-up men could get to her the horse bowed his head some more, Rose went to one side, he reached for her with his teeth and slapped her in the face with a hoof while she was still in the air. She never got to talk no more, not since she remarked that this was to be her "last ride." . . . Montana skies are blanketing her grave to day, with tears and smiles.

Marie Gibson, another Montana girl, went thru a contest with a broken jaw. A horse had broke it and she rode that horse again and a few others, just so she bring a little bacon home.

191

Mabel Strickland, a girl that would look just as well in a palace as she does on a horse, which is saying a whole lot, rode many a bucking horse and I noticed that her head popped less than the average cowgirl bronc rider. They tell me that Hugh, her husband, got crippled up some again, I hope I heard wrong, for Hugh was one of the best bronc riders and "dogger" I ever seen and I figured he might outlast Mike Hastings.

But Mike is hard to get rid of, he's the oldest cowboy in the game to day. He's been busted up and broke till there's nothing to him but a shell of gristle, bone and muscle, you ought to see that shell. Mike struts around like a gorilla, he can't help that, neither can the steer he lands onto. He always gets him down in fast time.

And, speaking of ropers, there's Chester "Chet" Byers the champion trick roper. Chet wins steady in trick roping with just a twist of the wrist, but that's some twist and his rope sure plays for him. Some feller wrote one time that the cowboy's work don't call for much exercise from the hips on up. I'd like to say a few words against that. I roped heavy stuff one day, the whole day long, in a corral and where I had to take dallies (turns around the saddle horn with rope) and before evening come my fingers was cramped to my rope so I had to knock 'em against the corral poles to leave loose of it and so I could make another throw. I'm not used to dallying and I was glad when the sun went down.

The average cowboy, specially the one who hasn't contested long, will do better roping on the range or in the corrals at the home ranch than he will in the Rodeo grounds. I've seen mighty fine ropers in the hills that wasn't so good in the Arena. That's on account they're not used to timing themselves and everything is strange, too many people around while in the Arena, then there's the rules to go by, the thought of having to catch, wrestle and tie the critter down in fast time so as to win something. . . . The critter is

I've seen mighty fine ropers in the hills that wasn't so good in the arena.

given a good lead, too good sometimes, and it takes a mighty fast and well broke cowhorse to take his rider up close enough to the spooked-up and dodging critter so the rider can make his throw.

In the bronc and steer riding events is where the cowboy don't get much chance to get stage fright. He's too busy keeping track of the twisting and hard hitting animal under him, and instead of worrying about making fast time he worries about staying on top and making a qualifying ride. That's to ride free and claw at the horse's shoulders and ribs with the taped spurs. Main strength rides don't go.

There's bronc riding with saddle and bronc riding bareback, with just a rope around the bronc's middle for the rider to hang onto. The big and wild longhorn Brahma steers are rode with just a rope too, and a noisy bell added on to spook him to do his worst. I seen a wild steer twist himself in such a way one time while bucking that he kicked a rider in the middle of the back while that rider was sitting straight up on him.

And with trick riding the rider has no time to pose and look pretty there either. For the cowgirls and the cowboys that's in that event are being watched by the judges, like the rest, and the way they fly around, under, behind and in front of a horse while he's at full speed you can't help but see that a feller sure has to know all about riding to be able to do them stunts. They sure make just riding around look strange.

Now comes the strangest, to the crowd in the grandstand, and that's the clown. He works all thru a performance and harder than any of the contestants, if he's a good clown. Red Sublette was about the best clown I ever seen, and what made him and other clowns strange to the people is because while he was dressed as a hayseed farmer, with goat whiskers and big boots he would do things in all events that was as good as the cowboys could do, only he done 'em in his own comical way. But Red Sublette is a mighty good all around cowboy, even if he did wear a hayseed outfit while clowning. I seen Red come out of the chute on some mighty tough bucking horses, anything that came along, he'd ride 'em backwards and whip 'em over the rump with his carpet bag at every jump they made. I seen him do everything that's done in Rodeos and do them mighty well, and then I'd hear somebody remark that "he was sure doing good for a hayseed." . . . Red has won many events in many contests. (A bronc just fell on him sometime ago and broke his shoulder and some ribs.)

There was a little cowboy who clowned in New York one year, Buddy Timmons. He wore a little derby hat, a tuxedo and played drunk, (he never drinks) and even after he showed his nerve and skill at clowning, after he'd played with them longhorn Brahma steers that was on the fight, rode tough broncs bareback and all the audience still thought he was some lounge lizard that was just playing smart. Even a cop thought so and came in the Arena, grabbed him and throwed him out, twice.

A-sitting up in the grandstand and looking down into the Arena the whole goings-on might look easy and showy. It's too bad that the folks a sitting up there can't come down and mix in. I know that many would like to, but that can't be done because the Arena would be too crowded and the cowboy would have no room to work in, besides there'd be lawsuits on account of some steer being careless with his horns or some bronc wicked with his hoofs.

The contesting cowboy don't pay much attention to the crowd that's around him. There's only three people he worries about and that's the judges. They're the ones who decide as to wether he wins anything or not, and wether he's going back home with his pickets a-jingling or empty. The cowboy is not a showhand. He comes to Rodeos to win whatever he can thru whatever he can do and he sees the audience only as an outside herd.

Only once in a while there'll be something come up that'll make him take his eyes away from the judges and the Arena for a short spell. . . . I know of one time when there was a narrow-brain standing away up to the top of the bleachers and hollering his head off as to how much better he could do than all the cowboys in the Arena. His hollering went on for quite a spell, he aggravated a lot of folks around and finally a cop went up to try and quiet him. He wouldn't quiet down, and as the cop started to reason with him this noisy hombre went a little wild. There was a cowboy sitting not far away, he heard the commotion, he'd already heard that feller speak too long to suit him, so, he went up and joined the cop and asked this noisy feller if he'd like to try his hand.

He was took down in the Arena and turned loose, and I'll never forget how quiet that feller got soon as he struck the sod. It was one thing to look down from a high seat, and another to be amongst the thick of the goings on. But he was game, even tho he was mighty ignorant of what he was up against. He asked for a horse, he got one, and that little easy bucking horse layed him in the stretcher and sent him to the hospital. It'd been too bad if he'd got a hard bucking horse.

You can't be a cowboy in a day, nor in a year's time. The good hand that comes to contest can show at least one generation of cowboy blood ahead of him, and if you'll notice the entry lists at any Rodeo you'll see the addresses of all contestants are from parts West where stock wears brands and never come home by call. There's more in being a cowboy than just be able to ride and rope, there's a spirit that goes with the life, a spirit of the kind that makes the cowboy do his dangerous work, go thru hardships in all kinds of weather, most of the time riding mean horses and for less wages than any other game or trade pays. His pride in being a top rider, roper and all around cowhand is what carries him thru, and out on the range as well as in the Arena there's a steady contest on that account. There's jealousy amongst the best and envy from them that ain't so good. Every man is for himself when there's contesting work to be done, and that's why when you see a Rodeo you see the squarest game that's played.

I never knowed of a case where a rider was bribed to fall off his horse or miss a throw so some other feller would get the prize, and as far as the bucking horses and steers are concerned it would sure take more than a whisper in the ear or a lump of sugar to make 'em lose any of their orneriness. The horses and cattle are range bred, the picked worst of what can be found.

A bad horse is like a bad man, he has that natural mean streak in him, and while the bad man winds up in close quarters with bars around the bad horse is carted around to different Rodeos and given all the chance in world to keep on with his meanness. He's fed all the strong feed he can eat and took care of as well as any thoroughbred race horse, the only difference is he don't get curried much, but he gets better than that and more according to his nature, for when there's no Rodeos for him to be at he's turned out to roll in good dirt and where hills are covered with tall grass.

On my ranch I had fifty head of bucking horses that'd been used at the New York Rodeo. Them horses didn't have a lick of anything to do for nine months a year but roam thru shady pines and tall grass, there was lumps of hard fat sticking out all over 'em, and as I rode by a bunch of 'em once in a while I could tell by their whistling snorts and the way they'd scatter that they sure stacked up on plenty more meanness. The riders that climbed aboard them horses as they was shipped to different rodeos didn't dare get half an inch away from their saddles when they came out of the chute on 'em or they was lost. The riders who stayed on and made a qualifying ride sure earned all the prizes they got, and ten times more.

I've heard some people remark that riding a bucking horse is all a trick. It's a trick alright, but it's all from natural talent and sense of balance, and plenty of experience. It's as much of an art as any art can be. I know many good cowboys that was born and raised in the saddle, rode most every day of their lives, long days, and could never get the hang of sitting a very hard bucking horse. Them kind of riders most always make up for that by being mighty good with the rope and savvying stock well.

About as good a rider as I ever seen was a little feller from Wyoming. A bucking horse had been the cause of his having a whole leg cut off, and with a wooden leg to take the place of it he rode circle all around many riders with two good legs. He was a born rider.

You seldom see a bronc rider or a bull dogger that ain't bunged up in many places, many get hurt every year and can't contest no more, and some get killed. After most every Rodeo there's a few left stranded in hospitals, without money nor friends and a long ways from the home range.

It used to be a few years ago that the peoples' and humane societies' sympathies was all for the horses and cattle and none for the cowboy. It was figured that Rodeos was unnecessary and just a plain show of cruelty to animals. On account of agitators the humane society investigated, there was a time when it looked like Rodeos was to be barred out of one state, but, as the humane officers got acquainted with the game that they didn't see where there was so much harm done to the stock as was imagined. They seen that the stock was in good shape and well took care of, they was showed and made understand how a Rodeo couldn't be put on if the stock was poor or weak or hurt, that it was to all advantage to have all animals in the best of condition, wild and ornery.

But to please the agitators there was some events left out, some was changed and new rules was made, and as it is now the animal has all the advantage and the cowboy none. The cowboy who contests these days sure has to be a wizard and an artist to win anything at the Rodeos.

In some states they won't let the Rodeo committee use the word "bull-dogging" in their programs and prize lists, that event's name was changed to steer wrestling. The reason for that was that some people thought bull-dogging meant turning some bulls into the Arena and then letting loose a bunch of bulldogs after 'em. If that had been the case I'm thinking that with them Mexican longhorns the bulldogs would of got the worst of it.

Bull dogging, or steer wrestling is where a cowboy rides alongside a full grown longhorn, and while at full speed falls on the steer's neck, grabs the horns and the tussle is on to throw him. It's some thrill to feel that steer's neck under your armpits, keep his horns out of your ribs as he tosses you around and while getting a holt of his

And the tussle is on to throw him.

head so as to twist it and bring him flat to earth. Sometimes a cowboy is drug plum around the Arena while Mr. Steer uses all his hoofs on every part of him.

The two events I like best in a Rodeo is the bronc riding (bucking contest) and the wild horse race. Most people like all events about the same, and that's good because they're sure all worth watching. But a good bucking horse always gets a stir out of me and always will. Such a horse gets a stir out of most anybody, so much with some in the grandstands that they want to try their luck riding one. I don't think there's ever been a Rodeo pulled off where there wasn't a few fellers asking for a chance to get to sit on one. Of course that's not allowed because the committee would be liable in case any got hurt, and it's only on special occasions and with special fellers that the committee might agree, and then with things special that way the fellers wouldn't be classed as contestants. If anybody is hankering to ride a bucking horse there's no use hollering that from a grandstand and trying to pose as a cowboy from up there. A cowboy never does that, he'll either go to the Rodeo headquarters and enter on the events he wants to compete in or else keep his mouth shut.

All entries are took in the day before the Rodeo starts, no later, and if any feller wants to try his hand at riding or roping that's the thing for him to do, enter thru the Rodeo office and get in the ring.

I've heard a heap about these Russian Cossacks, Arabians and others. Some people *write* me that they're better riders than the American cowboy, and still when Tex Austin went to Europe and put on a contest there, it took American cowboys to win the money every day in trick riding, and an American cowboy all the time in bronc riding, and every other event.

Anybody is welcome to enter in any Rodeo as long as the entrance fees are paid, I hear about so many different kinds of riders being so good, but I don't see hardly any names entered excepting them of the bow-legged breed that roams the Western ranges of the U.S.A. and Western Canada, and when the day of the finals come the prizes for Championships are awarded to nothing but cowboys whose homes scatter thru the West and from Mexico to Canada.

No matter now much a feller has rode, if he's never rode a bucking horse he's got something new coming there if he tries it. I'd advise an easy one at first, and he should never go to a Rodeo for any easy ones.

The Western horse has the blood of the wild horse in him, and the imported blood he's crossed with has only went to make him more of a fighter. He's stronger and more intelligent than the wild horse, and being free on the range he turns out every bit as wild as any mustang, I hear some folks remark after a bucking horse has been rode once that that horse would now be broke and never buck no more. Horses are all as different as people. Some will buck only once or twice and others will buck every time they're rode and as long as they live. I've got a mighty good saddle horse that was used in the Rodeos as a bucking horse for two years, and he was no slouch. He quit his bucking for no more reason than when he started it, he was just thru.

There'll always be bucking horses in the West. It's in the blood and in the air, and it's up to the men who contract to furnish bucking stock for the Rodeos to get the best of the worst of 'em. The horse has got to be a top notch bucker or he won't last in the Arena, if he fails to buck well just a few times he's soon replaced by one that won't fail, and that way a string of bucking horses makes the finest gathering of meanness there is in horseflesh. It sure takes a cowboy to ride 'em.

So, when you see a cowboy coming out of the chute don't think he's riding just a plain wild horse, he's riding one that took bucking to heart and made as much of an art of it as the cowboy did with his riding, and when you see a cowboy get bucked off don't think he's a poor rider, the best ones get bucked off once in a while. And if you'll read the rules that's in the programs and realize what a handicap the contestant is under so as to make a qualifying ride you'll wonder at the way the impossible is being done.

Now here's the last event, the wild horse race. By that I mean just what I say, a race run with wild horses and they're sure enough wild. They're unbroke horses shipped in from the range, not even broke to lead and the only way to get 'em into a chute is run 'em in from the corrals. Each horse is haltered in the tight chute, and when the whistle blows eight or ten of them wild ones are set free at once with two men a hanging on each halter shank. There's quite a commotion about now, some of the wild ones are running and bucking over other wild ones, saddles and riders and knocking 'em over. Finally some of the cowboys manage to get an ear holt, the others who are to race slip the saddle on, climb up in it and with only a rope and halter for racing bridle they all try to get their horses to the other end of the Arena first. Pretty near every horse is bucking in a circle and not getting to the other end, and the cowboy that's lucky enough to draw a horse that gets scared and stampedes is the one that wins the race. Some wild ones are bucking near all the way to the other end only stampede back without getting there.

The race is over now, so is the contest for the day. The wild ones are unsaddled, turned loose and run into the corrals. The crowd is standing up in the grandstand and beginning to file out, and the contestants in the Arena are waiting a spell, till the judges in the headquarters' office have added up the points for and against each rider, bull-dogger and roper. After a while they will go to the office, some will have won day moneys and there'll be many that will have not.

VIII

FOR A HORSE

Dusty Knight was a bronc peeler (bronco buster), and when that's said about him there's nothing to be took back, for he was at the top at the rough game. Dusty was also a lover, a lover of everything, and maybe that's why his lantern-jawed, Roman-nosed, and eagle-eyed face never agreed with the other features that was on it. Them other features made him look better than handsome.

Dusty had just been to town for about a week, his first time in many months. He'd showed his love for the cards there, lost all his money, and had to sell six of his eight horses so he could get back on his feet with the game. He got on his feet all right, won all his money back and quite a bit more, and then he went to show his love for what all pops under corks and places where fun could be got in a bunch. He loved all of that well, so well that he rode out of town broke.

But he still had his two top saddle horses and outfit, and now that he'd had his fun the range trails claimed him again.

Dusty was most always horse-poor, meaning that he always had more horses than he could use; he kept 'em in fine shape, and on one of his horses he could of rode anywhere with the best of 'em and felt proud. If he come acrost a horse that was an exception and to his taste, he'd dicker for him or work out the money in breaking other horses for him, but some way or another he'd get that horse. It was very seldom that he was left with only two saddle horses as he was now, but them two was his picked best, and few could touch them for looks, speed, and knowledge with rope and cow work. The other horses he'd let go, as good as they was, wasn't quite perfect to Dusty, and of course whatever little flaws they had wasn't found out till they was worked with a herd, maybe a week after he'd dickered for 'em.

Since his dad had took him on his first ride and before Dusty could walk, he'd rode hundreds of different horses, and always at the back of his head, seems like since he was born, there was the picture of one horse he had there, and with the many horses he rode and the thousands he seen he'd kept alooking and watching for that one perfect horse. He hadn't found him as yet; there'd been a little flaw that went against the mind picture he had in all of the best ones he'd picked on.

He was a couple of days' ride out of town, in the thick of good horse range, where he was always bound to be, and while riding through, going no place in particular, he zigzagged around quite a

He'd kept alooking and watching for that one perfect horse.

bit to always look over this and that bunch of range horses he passed near. Sometime soon he'd strike an outfit that wanted some horses broke; such a job was never hard to get, not for such a hand as Dusty was. He could prove his hand quick, too, by just watching him handle and ride one green bronc, just one; after that the job was his.

A job was his on his third day out. He'd struck a big horse outfit and where a man who could break horses well could always get a job. That outfit had plenty of horses to break, tough good ones, and it sure took a bronc-riding fool to line 'em out, because they was the kind that was born with a snort and raised with a buck.

Dusty done his usual fine work of lining out the first bunch, and then, when he run a second bunch in to start breaking, there was one horse in that bunch that come near taking his breath away. It was the horse he'd always had the picture of at the back of his head—the perfect one. The color of him was blood bay, black mane and tail, the blackest that Dusty had ever seen, and that horse's hide shined to the sun the same as dark blood that'd been polished on redwood. It was sure a pretty color. But that wasn't the only thing that agreed with Dusty's taste about that horse. There was the perfect built of him, from his little intelligent-looking head to his little hard hoofs. There was plenty of good body in between, about eleven hundred pounds of it, and all a proportion to what Dusty thought a horse should be.

"That's him, sure enough," says Dusty as he watched the horse snort and run around the corral, "and you just wait till I get his round back shaped to my saddle and his neck working to the rein, I'll be mounted like no king ever was."

Dusty was about right. But as perfect as the horse seemed to be, there was something about him that wasn't cleared yet. That was the brand on him; that brand showed that he belonged to another

"That's him, sure enough," says Dusty as he watched the horse.

outfit than the one he was working for, to a horseman by the name of Bill Huff, and Dusty figured he might have a little trouble fixing things so he could call that horse his own.

He was more than aching to start breaking him and see how he'd turn out, but breaking him would only raise the value in the horse, and so Dusty just broke him to lead, because now he was going to ride over and see the owner of that horse, Bill Huff.

He found out from the riders at the ranch that the horse had strayed. It was a good two days' ride to Huff's ranch, and Dusty, being wise to men's weaknesses for good horses, didn't take the horse with him as he saddled up one of his own and started over to see Huff.

Bill Huff had many horses; about half of 'em he would recognize by description; but when Dusty gave as poor a description as he could of that blood bay, he of a sudden perked his ears and didn't finish rolling his cigarette before he asked:

"Where did you see him?"

"Oh, about a hundred miles east of here. He's running with a bunch of wild horses and I'm thinking he'll be hard to get."

Dusty was lying, but most any honest man will lie when it comes to horses, even to his best friend.

"I just happened to be riding this way," Dusty went on, "and being I'm circling back now I could maybe catch the horse if you'll sell him cheap enough. I need a pack horse pretty bad."

"Pack horse!" snorted Huff. "Why, man, you'll never find the makings of a better saddle horse in your life. I'll give you fifty dollars to get him and bring him here to me."

That last gave Dusty something to think about. He seen that Bill Huff sure had no intentions of parting with that animal; he also seen how glad he'd been to learn the horse's whereabouts and the relief that he hadn't been stole. It'd been near a year since he's strayed away.

"Why, I wouldn't take five hundred dollars for that horse," says Huff, "even if he is wild and unbroke."

But Dusty had nowheres near given up the idea of getting that horse. He wasn't built that way. And it was while he was thinking hard and heard Huff say "unbroke" that he thought of a way.

"Have you any horses here you'd want broke?" he asks.

"Yes," says Huff, "quite a few, and the blood bay is one of 'em. Are you out for a job breaking horses?"

"If I can get enough horses to make the job worth while."

"I can rake up about thirty head easy, and if you're good enough hand I'll pay you extra for breaking the blood bay."

That went well with Dusty. With the scheme he had in mind, even though it would take time to put it through, he seen where sooner or later the bay horse would be his. He loped back to the outfit where he'd been working, drawed what money he had coming, caught his other horse and the blood bay, and in five days' time was back to Bill Huff's outfit.

There he went to work on the first ten head of broncs that was run in, and keeping in mind that he had to prove himself a good hand before he could get the blood bay to break, he brought out all his art at the game. The first few he started got the benefit of that, and in a easy way that made Bill Huff wonder, it seemed to him that them fighting broncs was no more than run in when the rough seemed to be took off of 'em overnight and a little girl could ride 'em. After a few days of watching such goings on, Bill decided that Dusty would sure do in handling his prize blood bay.

And Bill wasn't disappointed. Dusty took that horse, right away gave him the high-sounding name of Capitan before Huff could give him one, and was as careful of his hide as though it was made of diamond-inlaid gold lace. Capitan behaved fine for a green, high-strung bronc and bowed his head to buck only at the first few saddlings. He was quick to learn to turn at the feel of the hackamore rein, and his little chin quivered with nothing, seemed like, only by being anxious to tell ahead of time what was wanted of him and before the mecate knot touched the nerves of his jaws. His little pin ears worked back and forth as alive as his flashing eyes to what all was around him. Dusty still felt him to be the perfect horse, and to Bill Huff he was a dream that'd come to life.

All went fine for a week or so. Dusty rode the other broncs as their turns come, along with Capitan. And then, being Capitan was coming along so good, Dusty told Huff that he was going to turn him loose for a few days, that it would do the horse good and give him time to think things over; besides, he wanted more time to line out the other broncs so he would be done with 'em quicker.

Capitan run loose in a meadow of tall grass for a whole week, and, as Dusty expected and hoped for, that horse had accumulated a lot of kinks in that time. If that pony thought things over, it was towards how to buck good and nothing else.

It seemed that way to Bill, anyway. He was there when Dusty rode him time and again, and there hadn't been a one saddling when the horse didn't buck, and harder every time.

"Take it out of him, Dusty!" Bill Huff would holler, as Capitan would buck and beller around the corral. "Take it out of him, or, by gad, I'll kill him!"

That last would make Dusty grin to himself. He was now getting the horse to act the way he wanted him and so that Bill Huff wouldn't want him. Dusty would let on that he was also disappointed in the horse and act for all the world as though he was trying his best to take the buck out of him. He'd pull on the reins and slap with the quirt, and the pulls was easy and so was the slaps, and, at the side where Bill couldn't see, Dusty was only encouraging the horse to buck a little harder.

Capitan didn't need much encouraging; it was in his system to buck anyway, and he always felt like he had something off his chest when he done a good job at it. He'd been just as good in other ways and as a cow horse if that bucking instinct had been left to sleep, as it had before he'd been turned loose for a week; but after that week, and with Dusty giving him his head to do as he pleased while Bill Huff wasn't watching, he'd humped up and bucked a little. Dusty could of easy broke him off of that right then, but it was part of scheme to have him buck, and when Capitan didn't see no objections coming from his rider he fell into bucking in great style. Now it would take a heap of convincing by a mighty good rider to make him quit.

The horse was acting in great shape for Dusty, and Bill Huff had stopped coming to the corral when he was being rode. Bill had wanted that horse for himself, but he was too old to ride such as he'd turned out to be, and he was fast losing hope of his ever being of any use to him.

"He'll always buck," he says to Dusty one day.

Dusty had walked away and grinned. A few more days now and maybe Bill could be talked into selling the horse to him.

All was going fine, and then one day, before Dusty got to dickering for Capitan, a hammer-headed fifteen-dollar bronc bucked too high, and his feet wasn't under him when he hit the ground, but Dusty was. The horse had turned plumb over while in the air and come down on his back.

Dusty didn't come to his senses soon enough to talk to Bill about Capitan. When he come to he was stretched out in the back of an automobile and headed for town and hospital.

He laid in the hospital for a few months, wobbled around town for one or two more, and when he was able to ride again he hit for Bill Huff's.

Captain wasn't there no more, and Bill Huff went on to tell how it come about. When Dusty was laid up in the hospital he hired another bronc fighter to take his place and finish up on the batch of broncs that he'd started. That new feller was a pretty fair hand and he handled the broncs all right, all but Capitan. That horse had been loose for a couple of weeks and when he caught him he soon found he couldn't ride him. Capitan had kept agetting worse every time he was rode at. Other riders had tried him with no better luck than the first, and when there came rumors of a rodeo being pulled off in town, one of the boys was for taking that horse to it and let him buck there. He was entered as a tryout bucking horse, and he'd bucked so well that before the contest was over that horse had been promoted to a final horse, amongst the hardest of the buckers. Then Bill Huff had sold him as a bucker for two hundred dollars.

Well, it seemed like Dusty had sure done a good job in giving Capitan the free rein. He'd given him so much free rein that it now looked like he'd never catch up with him. But Dusty had nowheres near given up the chase. Capitan was the one horse in a lifetime to him, the one perfect horse, and of the kind he'd sort of lost hope of ever running across.

If he hadn't had the bad luck of a knot-headed bronc falling on him and laying him flat, Capitan would now be his instead of belonging to somebody else and being shipped from one rodeo to another as a bucking horse. It didn't matter to Dusty if Capitan had turned bucker; he was a young horse and he'd get over that. The main thing that worried him was if the new owner would part with him.

It wasn't many days later when he seen that new owner and found out he wouldn't part with Capitan for no love nor money. It was while a rodeo was going on, and when Dusty seen that horse buck he seen plenty of reasons why he couldn't be bought. Capitan had sure turned wicked.

Dusty was in a worse fix than ever towards getting that horse now. But he didn't lose sight of him. He followed him to two more rodeos, and his heart sort of bled every time he seen him buck out into the arena. That horse, he felt, was too much horse to be no more than just a bucker. It had been his intentions to take that out of him soon as he got him away from Bill Huff and make a top cow horse out of him; he had the brains and Dusty knowed he'd of made a dandy.

Being he hadn't as yet got over his injuries, Dusty didn't compete in the rodeos. He just stuck around. And one day it came to him to ask Tom Griffin, the owner of the bucking stock, for a job helping in the shipping and taking care of the bucking horses. He had to follow along to two more rodeos before he got that job, and by the time he worked at it for a month or so, Griffin was so pleased with Dusty that after the last rodeo of the season was pulled off he gave him the job of taking care of the bucking horses for the whole winter and till the season opened up again next early summer. Dusty was happy and felt he now had a mane holt towards what he was after.

Dusty was alone at a camp that winter. He had charge of sixty head of bucking horses and fifty head of Mexico longhorns that was used for bucking, roping, and bulldogging. The stock run out on good range, and in case of bad weather there was hay by the corrals for him to feed to 'em. He had plenty of grub and smoking and he was all set.

It was during that winter that Dusty went to doing something that made him feel sort of guilty. He was in good shape to ride again by then, and it would of struck anybody queer that knowed the bucking horses, more so Griffin, if they'd seen him pick on the worst one in the string, Capitan, and go to riding that horse.

But Dusty wasn't out for the fun of riding a bucker when he straddled Capitan; he was out to make that horse quit being a bucker

212

and make him worthless as such, and that's what made him feel guilty. He was spoiling his boss' best bucking horse by taking the buck out of him.

The only consolation Dusty had was by repeating to himself that there was lots of good bucking horses and that Capitan was too good to be one, and when the thought came to him that that horse would most likely be his after the first rodeo was pulled off, that sort of washed away all the guilty feelings he might of had.

Dusty about earned that horse before the hard bucking jumps at every saddling dwindled down to crow hops. Spring was breaking and Capitan still had plenty of buck in him, and any rider that could of went so far with such a horse was sure worth a heap of consideration, because few of 'em ever stayed over a few jumps while that horse bucked in the arenas. Of course there the riders had to ride by rules, and it's harder to sit a bucking horse that way than it is when there's no rules and all you have to do is stay on top.

By the time the snow all went away and the grass got tall and green, Dusty was using Capitan for a saddle horse, and what a saddle horse he turned out to be! As good as he'd been a bucking horse, and that's saying something. And now the only thing that worried Dusty was how Griffin was going to take it when he seen that horse come out of the chute and not buck, or would he go to bucking again? If he did there'd be no hope of Dusty ever owning him.

The day came when all the stock was gathered and preparations was made for the first rodeo of the year. Capitan didn't look like he'd ever had a saddle on that winter, and with the care that Dusty gave him—extra feeds of grain and all—he was as round and fat as a seal. Griffin looked at him and smiled.

But that smiled faded when that horse came out of the chute on that first rodeo, for Capitan just crow-hopped a couple of jumps and trotted around like the broke saddle horse he was. The cowboy hooked him a couple of times and all he could get out of him was a couple more gentle crow hops. That cowboy had to get a reride on another bucking horse so he could qualify. Dusty was just as happy as Griffin was surprised and disappointed. Griffin couldn't figure out how that horse quit bucking, for he'd expected him to be a top at that for quite a few years. He couldn't suspicion Dusty of having anything to do with it; he'd never seen Dusty ride and it would never come to his mind that any cowboy could take the buck out of such a horse, not when that horse had it in him so natural.

But Griffin wasn't going to lose hope of that horse ever bucking again. He put him in the tryouts twice a day. Capitan didn't at all do at first, but before the last day of the contest came it looked like he was beginning to turn loose and go to bucking again. Griffin begin to smile and Dusty begin to worry.

It was two weeks before time for another rodeo. In that time Dusty took charge of the horses again and held 'em in a pasture not far out of town. It was there that Dusty took the buck out of Capitan once more. It was easier this time because he hadn't accumulated much.

The same thing happened at the second rodeo as with the first. Capitan wouldn't buck, and every cowboy that came out on him wanted a reride, "on a bucking horse," they said, "not a saddle horse."

Capitan began to loosen up some more before the end of that second rodeo; but by the time Dusty got through with him the three weeks before the next rodeo that horse was scared to buck, and when that third contest did open up and Capitan couldn't be made to buck was when Griffin sort of lost his temper. The cowboys had been digging into him about bringing in gentle horses and trying to make bucking horses out of 'em, remarking that they was tired of asking for rerides and so on, till finally, when Capitan came out of the chute once more and only humped up as a cowboy hooked

It was there that Dusty took the buck out of Capitan once more.

him, he lost his temper for good and passed the remark that he'd take two bits for that horse.

Dusty was standing close by, expecting him to say such a thing.

"I'll do better than that, Tom," he says. "I've got fifty dollars in wages coming that I'll give you for him."

Tom hardly looked at him. He scribbled out a bill of sale and passed it to Dusty. Dusty folded the bill of sale, stuck it in a good safe pocket of his vest, and started to walk away. Tom sort of stargazed at him as he did, still dazed by the way Capitan quit bucking after every rodeo. Then, as he watched Dusty walk away so spry, the whole conglomeration came to him as clear as day. He was the one that wanted the horse.

"Hey, Dusty!" he hollered. Dusty stopped and looked back. "You're fired," he says.

"I know it," says Dusty, grinning, and walked on.

Capitan was led out of the bucking string of horses, saddled, and peacefully rode out of town. When the lanes was left behind and open country was all around, Dusty ran his fingers through the silky mane of the bay and says:

"All is fair in love as in war."

IX

TOM AND JERRY

TOM AND JERRY

I've often seen ponies pair off, form a pardnership and stick by themselves, fight for one another when there was need to, and scratch one another's itching withers in the shade of the big cottonwoods, plum contented to be away from other horses that's on the same range.

I'd most generally call them kind "Lone Wolves" on account of the scrap they'd put up when anything interfered or threatened to separate 'em.

A third party was as welcome as a rattlesnake and would be kicked out the same way, and if they happened to be rounded up and corraled along with other horses, they'd sure make it miserable for any other horse that'd come too close or try to nicker up an acquaintance. If one of the two got in a argument with a strange horse, and that strange horse was getting the best of him, his pardner would pitch in and help him till that stranger was boosted plum out of their sight.

That's the kind of pardners Tom and Jerry was. Them being full brothers maybe kinda accounted for it, but anyway they was sure *for* one another. By their color and markings and size you could hardly tell 'em apart; both was blood bays with one white hind foot and a star in the forehead, and as for their character they was both the same there too; one could be as ornery or as good as the other.

217

I'd paid twenty dollars for 'em when they was two-year-olds. Tom was four and Jerry was five when I run 'em in and started breaking 'em. I'd found 'em both wiry and full of snorts and between the two of 'em I'd got many a good shaking up, but it wasn't so long when their good sense came out on top, and when I got through with 'em, had two more good saddle horses to my string.

I'd always noticed when I turned 'em out on the range with other horses they'd been used to, they'd never seem to want to run with the bunch; instead they'd always branch off by themselves, and every time I'd want 'em I'd have to look in some other range from where my horses was running, and I'd never failed to find 'em all by their lonesome, either chewing on one another's mane or else feeding, never more than a few feet apart.

But I had no idea how strong their pardnership really was, till one spring I'd hunted high and low and couldn't find 'em nowheres. I'd got to thinking they'd left the country and went back to their home range which was to the north quite a ways. Then one day as I'm riding along and still watching for 'em, I spots a lone horse in the bottom of a coulee; he was running around in small circles and looked like he was chasing something. I couldn't make out just what he was chasing on account that I was too far away to tell—it could of been a colt or a calf, but what struck me to wondering was that whatever he was chasing would always turn around and come back to where that lone horse would make his stand.

I kept a low ridge between me and the spot where I'd seen the lone horse, and rode on a high lope to where I thought I'd be as close as I could get without being seen; then I rode over the ridge straight to where the commotion was taking place.

I recognized the lone horse to be Jerry soon as I got a peek at him—then I seen what he was chasing. It was a big gray wolf, and right away I could see that wolf wasn't figgering on being chased much longer; Jerry was near tired out and even though his hoofs was something that Mister Wolf had to keep out of reach from, that wolf knowed Jerry couldn't fight much longer, and he was getting braver all the time.

I sure cussed right there for not having my rifle with me, for I sure could of perforated that wolf right where he lived. I was too far for a sure shot with my six-shooter, but as I got off my horse and dragged myself through the tall grass towards him I had hopes that he'd keep on being interested in downing Jerry just long enough so I could get near.

Where could Tom be! I wondered, as I eased myself towards Jerry and the wolf. It came to my mind that maybe Tom had split up pardnership with Jerry and took up with other horses, but that didn't strike me as likely, and then I thought as I watched them two, how queer Jerry was acting. It seemed to me like he could of got away from that wolf if he wanted to, but, instead, every time he'd chase the wolf away he'd come back and stand in one spot and looked like he was waiting there for him to come again; the wolf would circle around but Jerry circled with him and stayed in the same place; when the wolf would come too close, that little horse would make a high dive for him and with flying hoofs, ears set back and teeth a-showing he'd make him scatter out of there.

But that wolf didn't scatter any too much; he'd just about keep his hide clear of Jerry's hoofs, and that was all, and I thought how lucky it was there wasn't another wolf to help him. The little bay horse would never had a chance then.

For as it was I could see the poor devil was near all in, every hair on him was wet with sweat and the way he was ganted up I knowed he hadn't had no water for a couple of days or more; he hadn't et anything either on account that there's no hankering for grass when a horse is real thirsty that way.

When the wolf came too close that little horse would make a high dive for him with flying hoofs.

What kept him from leaving that spot and going to water? I wondered; but my wondering was cut short by the wolf. He'd got wind of me when I was about a hundred yards from him, throwed up his head, sniffed the air, then put his tail where it wouldn't bother him and started traveling. I'd been watching for that move all the while I was edging in on him, for then is when I figgered would be time for me to act.

My "forty-five" spoke to him. Mister Wolf jumped in the air a good six feet, and when he landed I let another slug go his way, but none seemed to affect him outside that he was knocked over once. I fired at him till my gun was empty and each shot only seemed to boost him along to more speed till, when I straightened up and watched him top a ridge, I thought I seen him dragging one useless front leg.

Jerry was shaking like a leaf when the echo of the gunshots died down. Them shots had sure surprised and scared him, but he hadn't moved and was still holding down that one spot when I started towards him. I kept a-watching him to see what was the matter and the closer I got the more that little horse acted glad to see me. He'd nicker kinda soft, look down to one side of the spot where he'd been standing, and then look at me again.

I got to him fast as I could, and soon as I got there I seen the reason why Jerry hadn't tried to get away from the wolf, why he'd got along without water or feed, and why he stayed, fought, and protected that spot so well. A hole had been washed out by the snow waters and in that hole laying on his back, feet in the air and plum helpless was Tom—Jerry's pardner.

As I took in the lay of the things I figgered that Tom had been taking a roll for himself, and as luck would have it he'd picked on a bad place for such a purpose, with the result that when he rolled over he was too close to the edge of the hole and down in it he went.

That hole was only a couple of feet deep from the side where he started rolling but that was plenty to keep him there and the more he tried to get out the more he'd found himself wedged in to stay.

A horse can't live very long in that unnatural position, and as it was, poor Tom wasn't many hours from the end if left there, so I didn't waste no time. I made a run for the saddle horse I'd left on the ridge, and with my rope and his strength I soon got Tom right side up with care.

All the time Jerry was watching me, and when I finally got Tom's feet under him and where he could use 'em, he came to him, sniffed along Tom's knotted mane and nickered; Tom nickered back.

I couldn't do any more to help 'em so I just set there on the edge of the bank where Jerry had tore up the earth and stood guard over Tom. I watched the two ponies and thought a lot. I noticed Jerry staggering for the want of water—he'd fought hard and long to save his pardner from the jaws of the wolf, and now that all danger was over his nerves had relaxed and left him weak.

He stood there alongside of Tom and *waited* for him to get on his feet so they could both go to the creek together—the creek was only a mile or so away. Pretty soon Tom shows signs of interest in life and acts like he wants to get on his feet. I'm right there to help him all I can, and after working for a while and keeping on a-trying, Tom finally manages to stand on his legs. Mighty weak of course, but sure enough standing.

After that it was just a case of waiting a spell; then Tom takes one step, then another. Jerry is watching him all interest and when Tom indicates that he's going to keep on placing one foot ahead of the other Jerry catches up with him, and both a-staggering they head down the coulee towards the creek.

Yep, I says to myself as I watch the ponies move away—and Tom would of done the same for Jerry too.

JERRY'S ORNERY STREAK

That time when Jerry stood guard and fought the wolf away from Tom showed me a lot about what a real pardner is, and I never wondered since why them two was always together when loose on the range, and never would take up with any other horses.

I was the only one that ever butted into their company, I'd tried to make 'em my pardners the same as they was to one another and I think I finally got to where they'd tolerate me easy enough. Then come a time when it mattered a lot to me if them two sons of guns would do more than just tolerate my shadow, and finally, and after doing my best to get on the good side of 'em I noticed by Tom and his actions one day just how my standing was with 'em.

I'd just took the bridle off Jerry and was scratching him back of the ear, a mighty itchy spot right about that time, Jerry was enjoying it a lot and I was rubbing for all I was worth, when I noticed Tom coming along on the other side and nipping Jerry on the withers just as much as to tell him to get away. I kept a rubbing and watching Tom and then I got a hunch of what was going on in that pony's mind. He thought Jerry was getting altogether too much attention the while he was being neglected, in other words he was just plain jealous.

I got up to Tom then and started to make a fuss over him, that pleased him fine, but not so well with Jerry who gradually realized that he'd been left cold and seen where his pardner Tom was getting all the petting. He didn't like being neglected no more than Tom did and showed it by coming up and nipping him the same as he'd been nipped a little while before. . . . That was enough proof to me that from then on there was three of us, and all pardners.

Neither Tom or Jerry was what you'd call pets, I ain't got no use for that kind on account that they're always where they shouldn't be and doing what they shouldn't do, and to my way of thinking pets is spelled wrong, the s should be before the t and spelling pest, p-e-s-t.

To me a pet horse is a spoiled horse, and even tho Tom and Jerry liked me a heap and would nicker when they'd see me coming, they never was so gentle that they'd run over me to get a lump of sugar, they never stuck their nose in my pockets to look for such lumps or

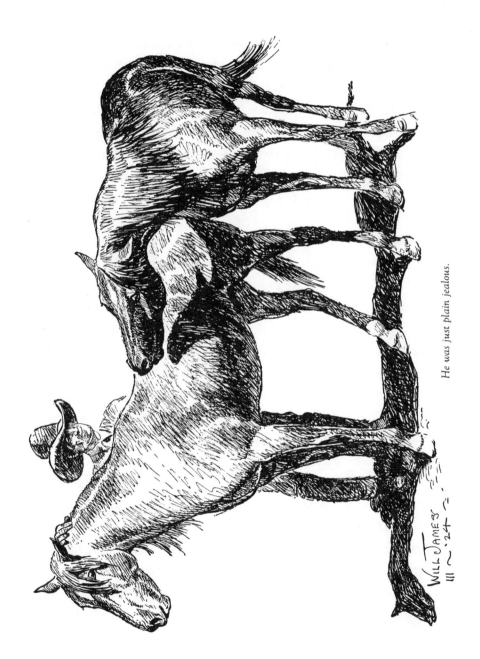

He was just plain jealous.

kick at me when they didn't get any, like I seen some pets do. Them two ponies didn't get no sugar, I didn't want to make fools out of 'em, but they got better than sugar for I always seen they had plenty to eat and lots of room to roll in. I kept no pinching shoes on their feet, nor founder 'em one day and starve 'em the next.

I savvied horseflesh and what was good for 'em, and they got to liking me for the breathing spells I'd give 'em, for the good range and green grass I'd turn 'em onto when spring came, and the warm sheds and good hay that was theirs when the cold winds and heavy snows would sweep over the ridges . . . and they got to liking me for my self too.

There was times when after running free for months and I'd corral 'em that they'd make themselves mighty hard to saddle and ride, the long sunny days of just picking over miles of good range for just the kind of grass that'd suit their perticular taste, and then just moseying along from one shade to the other and stopping at each shade long as they pleased on their way to a clear stream of water and all had spoilt 'em. It was hard for 'em to get back to work again.

And I wouldn't blame 'em none at all when after catching 'em and taking 'em away from all that, that they would try to buck me, saddle, and all off. I was right with 'em in that little scrap we'd have and I couldn't help but laugh at 'em when I'd see how ornery they'd act as I'd ride either Tom or the other out of the corral. Either one was like a kid (like some I know) that had a long vacation and then had to start for school again.

Jerry was a little the orneriest of the two and it'd take him longer to get the idea out of his head that he wasn't being treated right, he'd trot out with a kinky back, his ears pointed all directions but ahead, and what a cranky look he'd have in them eyes of his. I'd lean ahead in my saddle till my face was right alongside his head and kinda laugh at him, he didn't like to be made fun of, specially when

I was right with 'em in that little scrap we'd have.

he wasn't in good humor that way, and he'd always take advantage of such times to start acting up, just like a doggone kid again. But if he went too far and he wouldn't take the joke, all I'd have to do was talk to him a little, if my tongue was kinda sharp and he knowed I meant it he'd straighten up no matter how cranky he might of been.

For he remembered well how one day I'd spoke to him that way, and he knowed it was best to behave when he heard me use that tone, Jerry had been broke a couple of years then, I had him in a corral all by his lonesome. I'd put Tom in a big pasture with other horses, I'd sort of forgot *then* how thick them two was or I'd never tried to separate 'em that way, but I only needed one horse and I picked on Jerry. Anyway, I went out in the big corral to get him one morning and noticed as I'd tried to catch him that he'd developed an ornery streak thru the night. He'd look at me and snort like he'd never seen me before and tear around the corral as tho he'd never had a rope on him in his life.

I tried to walk up to him but I couldn't of touched him with a forty foot pole, then I got kinda peeved and went after my rope that was on my saddle. I was going to show him. . . . I shook out my loop, and when he made a wild dash past me I let it settle down around his neck and pulled up my slack.

As a rule Jerry had always been pretty good on stopping and facing me soon as the rope touched his neck and he knowed he was caught, but that morning he was an altogether different horse and instead of behaving when he felt the rope he seemed to get all the wilder. A tornado was slow compared to him and the way he went around that corral, I tried to get my end of the rope around the snubbing post but I'd always find it short a few feet, and I'd cuss the hombre that'd built such a big corral.

In the meantime that horse was getting worse every minute, talking to him with the idea of quieting him down didn't do no good, and then all at once I seen what he was going to try next, that was to jump over the corral. There was nothing I could do but watch every move he made and catch him at just the right time when he'd try that stunt. I was going to try and queer him at it.

I hung on to the end of the rope while Jerry was going around me like the devil was after him. He acted as tho he had a fit, and he didn't seem to hear me as I called his name, there was no quieting him at all, and pretty soon that corral, as big as it was, got too small for him.

I could tell he was going to jump by the way he looked over the top of it and started, I was ready . . . I called his name again as he went up and over, I wanted him to remember that call, at the same time I run on the rope with him till my chance come, and when his four feet was off the ground and he was starting down on the other side I gave the rope a flip, let it run thru my fingers a couple of feet and then set down on it.

That done the work, the leverage I had along with the horse off all his four feet that way all done the trick of setting him right on end and head down, and when he landed on the other side it sounded like a ton of brick had just fell out of the sky.

I hated to be that rough on the little horse but it was a case of where I had to, many good ponies turned outlaws for winning out in an ornery streak that way and I couldn't let Jerry get by with it on account I knowed if he did he'd try it again, and besides I wanted to get within touching distance of him so I could find out the cause of his acting up that way.

Jerry layed there on the other side and all out of wind, that'd been knocked out of him in the fall and when I got to him and slipped the hackamore on his head I could tell the way he looked at me that he'd be good from then on. His good senses had been jarred back to full use.

He never knowed what had stopped him so sudden, turned him over so quick, and layed him down so hard when he jumped that corral, but I could see he understood that his getting busted that way had something or all to do with when I hollered his name for him to behave. He knowed he'd been doing wrong and that he should of listened to me, . . . and that's why from then on, and no matter how ornery he wanted to get or how he wanted to tear things up, all I had to do was use that tone I used that time, and just say "Jerry" and that little horse calmed down to what he really was, a good horse.

It wasn't fear that made him behave either, for even tho Jerry knowed I could *make* him be good he had no fear of me, I didn't treat him that way but instead I worked to get his confidence, and I had it. I was careful to hide that I was his master excepting in times when he needed straightening out like I've just told. Outside of that I was a pardner of his the same as with Tom. We worked *together*, and I didn't *make* him do a thing, just showed him what was to be done and let him go ahead, and always he'd try his best to see what a good job he could do at whatever was pointed out to him. . . . The big rowels on my spurs would turn out as just ornaments, I'd have no use for 'em none at all.

It was a few months later when I found out what was the cause of Jerry's acting up and jumping over the corral the way he did. It had come to me that him and Tom had never been separated from the time they was colts, they'd followed the same mammy, and then I knowed right away that Jerry had just fretted hisself over being separated from Tom, till when I came to catch him the next morning he wasn't at all the same horse.

That made me feel kinda bad too when I thought how I stopped him, and worse yet when I seen how I misunderstood the little horse, and figgered his actions to be just an ornery streak . . . but that misunderstanding caused us two to realize a lot. Jerry seen I wouldn't stand for no foolishness, and it all gave me a peek at the strong heart that pony was packing. . . .

WILL JAMES
'30

SCATTERED THREE WAYS

I'd had mighty hard luck that summer and when fall come and winter settled in, I'd only put in three months work instead of eight as I usually did. That hard luck started early in the spring, and came along in the shape of a five year old bronc a feller wanted me to break for him.

That bronc wasn't at all honest in his fighting, he'd throw himself backwards, forwards, or any old way that he could so long as he'd get you under. And one day he did.

I had doctor's care for a couple of months, layed around and recuperated for two months more, and after putting the finishing touches on the bronc that did all the harm and making a good horse out of him, I run in my two ponies, Tom and Jerry, and started out to join the wagon which was already out on fall round up.

The money I made there went to pay the doctor that'd took care of me and when the wagon pulled in and the work was all done I still owed seventy dollars. I rode into the little cow town with the idea that I might run acrost somebody who wanted to hire a bronc fighter and where I could clear enough dinero to put myself in the clear.

But that was a hard country to put in the winter, and I soon found it out. Riders was drifting in and looking for a steady winter job the same as me, and none seemed to be going out, but most of 'em was in better fix than I was, they had their summer's wages with 'em and could afford to wait, where with me I had to borrow a little. Then them two ponies of mine eating good hay in the livery stable sure didn't help matters any. Their board bill was getting high, and I was beginning to do some tall wondering how I was going to get out of there.

Then one morning, I stepped out from the hotel and headed for the stable still scouting around for work and at the same time say "hello" to my two ponies. On the way over I met up with my doctor, and him and I walked along together. He went in the stable with me just to be sort of sociable, and followed me out to where Tom and Jerry was taking life easy.

"Them is fine ponies you got there," he says as he spots 'em, "are they gentle?"

"Yes," I says, "they're gentle enough."

"Gentle enough for me?"

"Well, I don't know," I says looking at him quick, "nobody's ever rode 'em but me."

"You know," he says looking straight at them ponies, "I used to ride quite a bit and lately I've been getting the idea that I'd like to have a good horse to lope out with once in a while, just for the exercise."

And pointing to Jerry he asks, "Would you sell that one?"

I had no time to answer for he follows up right away with "Saddle him up for me will you, I'd sure like to try him."

I didn't like the idea of him getting on Jerry no more than I did of refusing him, the doctor had been daggone white to me, and it was hard. But one glance at him decided me and I went and got my saddle.

Jerry sure had a queer look in his face when he seen who was climbing up on him, but he was took by surprise and seemed like he wasn't getting over it very fast. Tom had his head up and watching things pretty close too, and I knowed he was sure doing his share of wondering.

In the meantime, the doctor was riding Jerry around the corral and watching out for his fine points, how well he reined, how quick he was on his feet, and how proud he carried himself. I could see he was tickled to death with the horse, and before Jerry had come out of his trance and realized a stranger was on him, the doctor climbed off and backing away to the end of the bridle reins, stood there and looked Jerry over for blemishes he might have.

"Clean as a whistle," he says as he turns my way. "And I'll tell you what I'll do. I'll give you a hundred dollars spot cash for that horse or else let me keep the seventy you owe me and give you thirty, then we're square. But I'll do any way that suits you, only I'd sure like to have him."

A hundred dollars was a mighty good price for a horse Jerry's size, but then again that same amount meant nothing if it came between me and that little horse, and what's more I had no hankering of ever parting with him. Him and Tom meant more to me than just money even tho I was broke and owed a little.

But hard facts made me get down to bed rock and showed where I had to forget my sentiments for a spell. I had to do something soon or else I'd have to leave both of my ponies to pay for feed bills, mine and theirs. Getting a job in town was past me, and being none of the stockmen around seemed to be wanting any riders, I figured the best way for me was to clear out and head for another country. I'd only have one horse to do it with and I'd have to leave my gatherings behind but that I thought was a heap better than being afoot, and then I figured sometime I could maybe buy Jerry back again, he'd have a good home here too, but there was still one hope.

"I'm afraid," I says, "that horse might be a little mean for you soon as he knows a stranger's got him."

But I was only laughed at for that remark and as the doc said,

"I know a good gentle horse when I see one, and besides I've rode quite a lot myself, young feller, don't forget that."

That ended me right there, and seeing how he wanted the horse and how it was my only way out, I just had to quit and say,

"All right, he's yours."

As a rule I could take either Jerry or Tom and ride out for a day's ride leaving one behind without him making a fuss, both was used to that and if I rode out on Jerry, Tom knowed I'd be back with him before sundown and there was no trouble. But as I caught Tom and talked to Jerry a spell before leaving I could see them two wise ponies had caught on right away as to what was up.

Tom wasn't at all for going *straight* out of town, he'd zigzag and want to turn back and I was finding it a mighty hard jolt on my feelings when I had to persuade him to keep on ahead. He'd nicker back at the pardner that was missing and that didn't make me feel good either, for I knowed, even tho we was too far to hear, that there was another little horse back there answering and a calling.

*He'd nicker back at the pardner that was missing
and that didn't make me feel good either.*

I rode out thirty-five miles or so that day, and there wasn't a foot of that distance that wasn't hard work. That little Tom horse had no heart left in him, and that long ground eating gait of his I liked so well had disappeared, and instead he was just a jogging along like them leg-weary livery plugs, chopping each step to half, keeping his ears and eyes on the back trail, and nickering along every so often as he went.

It was hard on him, and he sure made it hard for me too. I was glad when dark came and I turned into a lane leading into a ranch figuring on stopping there for the night. And a heap gladder when that night and after supper I was asked if I was wanting work and willing to take on a few head of broncs.

Willing? . . . why godamighty, I'd took on the devil himself right then and his whole tribe, and made little angels out of the whole kaboodle right in their own territory, all for two bits a head. Here I'd stumbled onto a good job just when I thought there was none in the country, sixty head of colts to break which meant enough work for eight or nine months, at sixty dollars per month. (Mighty good wages for them days.)

Right away I thought of Jerry, I was going to get him back, and I wasn't going to wait till I'd earned the hundred dollars either, I was going to get it in advance this time. The foreman had seen my kind often thru the cow countries, and he understood how it was when a cowpuncher gets married to his ponies that way. He savvied and never hesitated to advance me the hundred.

The next morning found me up before the cook opened his eyes, and making sure the check was in my pocket I headed for the stable to saddle up Tom, but Tom?—he was gone, that son-of-a-gun had left. Part of the rope that'd held him was still on the manger all chewed up, I could see where he then scouted all thru the big stable and finally had found a crack in a door, some of his hair was enough evidence that he'd made that crack bigger and worked himself thru. Then I went to the lane where we came in the night before and there was Tom's tracks. They showed plain how fast he was traveling and where he was headed.

I caught me a company horse and a little after noon that day I rode up to the Doc's home, there I learned that Jerry had made a get away too, and then I got the whole story of what all had happened. First, and after I left town that morning, the doctor had saddled Jerry up and was going for a ride. But Jerry couldn't see it that way, and he just proceeded to buck him off.

"Twice he done that," says the M. D., "and after I seen there was no use me trying him, I just pulled the saddle off of him."

Twice he done that," says the M. D.

"I'm glad you came," he goes on, "and by the way, I'm wondering if you'd want him back, because sometime last night, I don't know just when, but anyway he got away, I just missed him this morning so I don't think you'll have a hard time finding him."

I clinched the deal right there and give the hundred, Jerry was my horse again. I rode to the livery stable where Jerry had been. The stable man was all puzzled and said he couldn't account for Jerry's getting away.

"The gate was opened from the outside," he says, "and I know that Jerry horse couldn't of done it."

I was doing some tall grinning as I rode out of town and a few miles further started to cut for tracks, it was just as I figgered, and I

They both turned, faced me with their heads away up, and nickering came to meet me.

wasn't at all surprised when pretty soon I runs across two horse tracks in the snow, fresh tracks and headed straight for Tom and Jerry's home range, a couple of hundred miles to the south.

It was near dark when riding on a high lope, I finally caught up with 'em. They started to run as they seen me, but soon as I talked to 'em, they both turned, faced me with their heads away up, and nickering came to meet me and stopped. . . .

"Well now," they seemed to say, "being that we're all together again, where are we going from here?"

And as I turned 'em towards the ranch and the steady winter job I noticed Tom lining out again with that long ground covering gait of his once more.

I never wondered how that corral gate was opened from the outside, for I knowed from the start that Tom was the guilty party, but his conscience never bothered him any.

WILL JAMES
'30

But the cowboy had turned his head.

X

SCATTERED TRACKS

Wild-eyed, snorting at every jump, an empty and blood-stained saddle on his back, a big gray horse was pounding granite gravel into dust as, in a high lope, he wound his way up along a brush-covered ridge. He'd just got rid of a rider a few minute before. Queer thing, too, that rider wasn't bucked off; he'd just went limp and gone down of his own accord, seemed like. The horse had "spooked up," at that, kicked at the man as he fell, and run on; and now, every once in a while, as a dry oak limb would "goose" him on the neck, he would go to bucking and try to get the saddle off.

And he was doing pretty well; the saddle blanket finally slipped out, leaving the saddle all the looser; and finally, with every bucking spell, it started to turning. When he came out of one patch of scrub oaks it was well on his side; and as he came out of another, it was under his belly. He got all the more scared then, and proceeded to try and kick the hunk of leather to pieces as he stampeded out of one patch of brush into another.

It'd been just a little after sundown when he got rid of his rider, and he'd stampeded and bucked and kicked from then on till away into the night. The sky was starting to lighten up in the east when he begin to let up, but there wasn't much left of that saddle by then: the stirrups had both been kicked off, and the stirrup-leathers had been tore loose from the saddle tree; the skirting was all pawed to frazzled edges, and very little was left but the tree, the riggin' and the cinches.

With that little to hinder him, he'd cooled down some and begin to get used to it. After a while he went to grazing a little, and then, with all the exertion he'd went through, he got to hankering to stick his nose in a pool of water somewhere.

That's how come that the early morning sun found the big gray horse by the troughs of the Maxwell ranch. He'd drank his fill, and now he was standing with head down and taking in the sun's warming rays.

From the little ranch-house that was up the hill a ways there came sounds of a door opening, but them sounds came from too far for the horse to hear, and he never cocked an ear.

"Donna!" It was a man's voice calling. "Ain't that Scorpion out there by the troughs?"

A woman came from the kitchen stove to the door, and as she looked out, she sort of clutched her apron, for she at once noticed the saddle, what was left of it, a-hanging under the horse. To range folks, such a sight hints to a serious happening; and more so to Donna, for it hadn't been but a year or so before when that same horse came in to the troughs in the same way, with a saddle hanging under him. Her husband, Dale, had been bucked off and stomped on, and left out in a tangle of boulders and brush. The happening had left him paralyzed all down one side, and he'd been riding a wheel-chair ever since.

She was speaking to him now, and she clutched her apron all the more as she thought of what might of happened this time, to someone else. "Gee, Dale," she says, "it looks as if somebody has tried to ride that horse.

Breakfast didn't amount to much that morning. Donna went to looking for some bandages, anything that'd hold a human together till he was brought into where he could be took care of proper. She gathered some food to take along, filled a canteen full of water. Then she kissed her husband, and patted his good arm, smiled some Injun sign language for him to wheel himself around and cook some hot breakfast, and away she went.

The troughs was right by a big corral; the gate was always open there, and it was no trick for her to haze the big gray horse in. Without a glance at him, once he was in the corral, she went and got her rope and flipped a neat loop over that pony's head, snubbed him, and then flipped another loop around both his front feet; then she took the saddle off and examined it, but there wasn't much left about that saddle which would tell any story—nothing only spattered blood-spots on the fork, and that made things some mysterious, because as a rule, a hurt from a horse don't usually draw blood. Hoofs can mangle a body without breaking the skin.

Donna didn't waste much time looking at the saddle. One glance at it had been enough to tell her all she wanted to know. In a few minutes she had two horses up from the little wrango-horse pasture, and soon, leading one extra horse, she was cutting for the tracks the big gray had made.

Tracks had been Donna's first A. B. C's with her dad; she'd first learned to track wild horses, wild burros, moss-horn Yaks, mountain lion, and near every animal that roamed that rocky, brushy southern country. Tracks and signs had been her grammar; and later on they got to be her book of life, of happenings. Through them she knowed a lot of what went on in her little territory; and since the accident to her husband, she got to reading them the same as the town man reads his morning paper.

But with her it was for the whole day along, for now she was doing all the riding. The few hundred head of cattle which was theirs kept her in the saddle steady, and if she did put on an apron once she got home, it was always over a riding skirt. She had no use for house slippers no more—riding boots had took the place of them.

The work was hard for her sometimes, too; there was things that she, or no other woman, could do very well—like branding, for instance, or breaking a bronc' to saddle; and if it wasn't for a few cowboys dropping in on her once in a while to help her out that way she'd been sort of up against it, because she couldn't afford to hire any help, not till that bunch of cattle Dale had mortgaged his holdings to buy was paid for.

"It's too bad there ain't a bounty on them," says a cowboy who'd come to help Donna one day, "—say, about a nickel a head. I know where I could make about thirty cents in five seconds."

Donna had smiled. "No use feeling that way," she'd said. "If Dale was all right, everything else would be that way; or if our little Jimmy had lived——"

She'd kept on smiling as she said that last, but the cowboy had turned his head.

Little Jimmy—here was another whose fate she'd read by tracks. It was by them that she'd seen where he'd tangled with a big old "moss-horn." The boy had got mixed up with that critter, a cat-claw, and the bronc' he was riding. He'd just turned sixteen, and he was tough. He felt all right at the time of the happening, and he never told his mother nothing about it, nothing only that he'd got his rope on a bullock and lost him; but later a blood-clot formed in his brain, and he went where all cowboys go. That should be heaven.

That was a little while before Dale left tracks of *his* happenings in the 'dobe and granite dirt; and with that last one, Donna couldn't see tracks no more for grief, not for quite a spell; but soon a lot of work came up which had to be done, and riding to the breeze every

Nothing only that he'd got his rope on a bullock and lost him.

day sort of aired her mind and dried her tears—tears which nobody got to see.

Then one day the "Scissor" round-up wagon came along and camped at a spring near her place. There was over twenty cowboys with the spread; one of 'em was layed up and suffered with a broken leg—he'd been found by tracks too. And Donna, like as if she didn't have enough to do, went to work and took care of him. She insisted they bring him to her house. . . .

Now she was on the trail again, following and reading horse-tracks which told of another happening. She didn't wonder how come this rider to be riding one of her horses, that he might of stole him, and so on.

She came to where the big gray horse had grazed, rode straight on through them tracks to where she figgered he'd come, then later on, found signs of where the saddle had first turned under the horse's belly. The rider shouldn't be far now.

She rode on and on, never thinking of the food and water she'd brought along. The sun wasn't far from tipping the western ridges, and still she rode, all eyes and strained face on the tracks ahead. It was near dark when, of a sudden, the wide and scattered tracks of the stampeding, bucking horse narrowed down to a straight, even gait. She stopped her horse.

"Right here," she thought, "is where it must of happened."

But she couldn't see no sign of any rider nowhere. The place was in a deep arroyo; in the bottom of it was ledges of rock where the water had washed over and scooped out holes underneath.

She got off her horse and begin to look under the ledge where he was most likely to be; and there all huddled in a knot, one hand over his belt and covered with blood, the other hand on a long-

barreled six-shooter which pointed straight at her, was the rider she
was looking for.

"Aw, hell," was the greeting she got, as the rider seen Donna's
long hair hanging over the edge of the ledge, "it's a woman!"

Donna never seemed to hear the remark, nor notice the gun which
had been pointed at her; all she seen was the pain in the man's face,
the position he was in, and the shirt and hand that was full of
blood.

She got up, went to her horse, untied the food and canteen of
water which she'd brought along, and hurried back to the wounded
man. Laying back in his hole like a cornered wolf, the man watched
her come; and Donna was mighty surprised and hurt when, with
motion of his good hand, he held her back with all she'd brought
him. No one, not even Donna, could of realized what an effort it
was for him to do that just then, and she only wondered why he
refused what she thought he'd be needing the most.

But she wasn't to wonder long. "No ma'am," he says, "I never
done no good by nobody, and I don't want anybody to do good by
me. All I want is to be left alone, just for a little while——"

His hand dropped as he spoke them last words, and the gun fell
by his side; then he started to speak some more, but it was near
impossible for Donna to make out what he said; and what's more,
she wasn't worried as to that: she only realized that he was in a
delirium and badly in need of care.

It wasn't a bad horse that'd done the harm this time; it was hard-
nosed bullets. His back and right side had been punctured by four
of 'em, and that she found out soon as she seen that the man had
gone unconscious. Donna had never treated a bullet-wound, but
she done her very best; and by the light of a brush fire she'd made,
managed to doctor him up in pretty good shape. All her bandages

went for that purpose, and in a few minutes she had him trussed up so that very little of his hide showed.

She was wiping his face with water when he stared around at her and begin to speak again. "There's no use, ma'am," he was saying. "No good'll come to you for this, and—I wish you'd leave me alone."

"Now, you keep quiet," says Donna. "I'm handling this. You're going to drink some of this water now, and eat a little, and then you're going to ride to the ranch with me."

"Yes, and be turned over to the——"

The rider stopped short with the last word, but Donna knowed just what he was going to say. If that mattered to her, she never showed it, and she went to feeding and taking care of the man the same as if he was a Jimmy or a Dale. After a lot of persuading, she finally got the canteen to his mouth, and then she had a hard time taking it away from him, for with the first drop of water, he'd went wild for more; but she managed to get the canteen away from him, and then forced him to take a little food.

"If you're bound to do something for me," he said after that, "just leave me the water. I ain't got far to go, and that'll be all I'll need."

But she didn't pay no attention to his talk. "Now, just put your good arm over my shoulder," she says, as she kneeled down, "and I'll help you up. Don't be afraid to put your weight on me now—come on; I've got to get you home."

There was no use arguing with her; and the rider, as much as he wanted to hang back, found himself doing just as she wished. With her help he got out from under the rock ledge and stood up; and then he tried to maneuver by himself. To him, a woman was just a creature to admire from a distance, and not to lean onto—they might break.

But Donna didn't break. She hung on to his good arm and proved mighty strong as she helped him toward the horse. She proved still stronger as she boosted him into the saddle; and the rider, through shame of being helped by a woman that way, near forgot his hurts. He resented the whole thing, this being helped and all, specially by a woman. Nobody had ever helped him before—they'd all tried to stomp him down; but he'd somehow stood under all of that, got used to it, asked no favors and gave none. He'd been a lone wolf and gave 'em all a merry chase; now he'd reached the end of his string and he would of been pleased to just cash in without anyone raising a hand.

The ride back to the ranch seemed a mighty long one, as much to Donna as to the man; they could just poke along, and once in a while, when he'd get in a delirious spell, she'd have to stop. It'd take all her strength to keep him in the saddle then.

Lucky, she often thought, that they was traveling in the cool of the night. Maybe they could get to the ranch before the sun got very high, if the man could stay in the saddle that long. He hadn't said a word since they started; she wished he would, because that'd give her some inkling as to how he was making it, but the rider had his reasons for not speaking.

They still had eight or ten miles to go when the sun appeared over the eastern ridges. The rider was slumped in the saddle. Pretty weak, when a rider like him does that, thought Donna. He'd had no more delirious spells for quite a while now, but instead, he seemed to be in a trance, like as if he was half-unconscious. Donna rode close by him so as to catch him in case he started to fall off; and she seen that the only way he kept in the saddle was through the knack every cowboy develops after many years spent in that rig. He'd rode there even if he'd been dead.

They was just a few miles from the ranch, and the sun was getting high and hot, when Donna spotted a rider coming their direction. For her own reasons, she hoped this rider was a cowboy; and sure enough, when he pulled up to howdy and raised his hat, she seen he was riding a Scissor horse, a spooky one, and he sat him like any good hand does. But she didn't know this man—must be a new one on the outfit. That didn't seem to matter, though, not to the cowboy anyway, because he acted like he sure enough knowed her, and he did—he'd heard of Donna a plenty from the other boys.

That respectful look of his proved that, and his eyes, after resting on the crippled man a second, only asks if he could be of service.

Donna was quick to understand that look, and as quick to take him up on it. "I'm Mrs. Maxwell," she begins. The rider nodded and went on listening for more. She went on: "I've got a man here that's hurt bad and will need a doctor as soon as possible. Could you go to town, or telephone in from the Barclay ranch, and get one for me? I can't get away."

"I'll sure do that, Mrs. Maxwell." The rider started to ride away, then seeing Donna had more to say, he brought his fidgety horse to a stand again.

"I just wanted to ask, that if you have any suspicions of this man, or know of him, you will keep it to yourself and won't say anything to nobody about your seeing him."

"I sure wouldn't," says the cowboy, "even if you hadn't asked."

And sure enough. A hot branding-iron on that cowboy's ribs couldn't of made him tell. No words would of come out of him, only maybe them a cowboy uses when he's riled up.

Dale Maxwell had wheeled himself on the porch. He'd been there since the break of day, and watching down the little valley for a dust or a moving speck that'd tell him of Donna's return. He'd got pretty anxious and sort of worried, long before he spotted the dust her pony's hoofs stirred, and soon as he could make sure of that, he wheeled himself back into the house, and from his chair, started a fire, put on a pot of coffee, and went on to dig up more to cook, all of which would go mighty well after her long twenty-four hour ride.

All was ready and pushed back where it'd keep warm, when he heard horses' hoofs, and spurs jingling, and a second afterward the tired but smiling face of Donna appeared at the door.

"I've got him, Dale," she says. "Don't know who he is—hurt pretty bad, and I have to bring him in the house right away. Don't go to fretting, now—I can do that easy." Then she was gone.

But Donna knowed it wouldn't be an easy job to get the hurt rider into the house; he was limp as a sack of meal, and it took a considerable lot of maneuvering to get him on the porch. Dale had wheeled himself to the door and cussed his own helplessness.

"If you'll help me on another chair, Donna," he suggested, "you could maybe get him in this one; then you can wheel him in."

It took over an hour to get the rider in and dress his wounds again, and Donna felt pretty weak herself by then; but it wasn't till then, and after her thirsty horses was took care of, that she finally come in and took on some of the hot coffee and food her husband had fixed for her.

"Better get a little rest now, Donna," says her husband, after she got through eating. "I'll watch him for you, and wake you up if you're needed." There was no more she could do, not with the injured man. Of course there was plenty of riding, and little chores to be 'tended to around the place, but that would have to wait. It was middle afternoon when her husband came in to wake her up. He sure hated to do that, but he seen a buggy coming—the team was in a high lope. It was the doctor.

"That cowboy sure didn't waste much time," thought Donna, as she hurried to dress. It was forty miles to town, and only half of that distance could be covered by an automobile.

It was a great relief to have the doctor come. Donna made a mighty good hand of herself as a nurse. The rider was in a trance as the bullets was extracted, and he talked a whole lot. Too much to please Donna.

"I hope you won't remember what this man said," she says, as the doctor was making ready to leave. "Maybe it's wrong for me to feel this way, but he's mighty young; besides, he couldn't be moved very well, could he?"

"It would kill him to move him," says the doctor. "I'm very doubtful if he'll live, anyway. He might if nothing sets in, and as far as what I heard him say is concerned, you won't have to worry about me telling. My profession is to heal people."

As Donna sat by the bedside of the wounded man in the couple of days that followed, she listened to a lot more which she'd rather not heard. As Dale took his turn watching over him, he heard a lot too, and the two talked it over afterwards in low voices, and like as if they was in cahoots with the hunted outlaw. For that's what the man was. His talk told of hold-ups, cattle- and horse-stealing, and smuggling stolen stock acrost the Mexican border. But as his talks was pieced together, it was found that his being an outlaw wasn't because he lacked other ambitions or because he was naturally a thief. He mentioned men's names, men he'd shot at off and on, and as he'd often say, "I wish I'd killed the damn skunks now, and had it all over with."

It seemed that them men had had all to do with giving him a bad name which he didn't deserve. Everything that happened that was bad, and for a hundred miles around, had been fastened onto him. He'd been wild, and them happenings was easy fastened, and with the name he packed, he couldn't begin to prove his innocence. He could of left and went to new territory, of course, but he wasn't the kind that'd run, not from anything.

So he'd stuck, and getting sort of soured at everything and every-body in general, he'd went the limit to make it interesting. Nobody was any good, and he was no good either; but he was getting some consolation out of making it hot for his enemies, and that's what had kept him going.

Donna seen through that, more so, on account of her being a woman, than Dale could. She remembered her own son, little Jimmy—this man reminded her of him, sometimes, the way he squinted into space; and she felt like he just ought to be spanked and finish that off with a good big hug.

But it took Donna to be inspired that way, for with a glance at the lean unshaved jaw of the rider, his hard, cold eyes, eyes that seemed to fit in only with the sights of a six-shooter, few others could of thought of any good in the heart of him. Maybe, with Donna, it was because she found him at the end of scattered tracks, like she'd once found her Jimmy and Dale.

The next few days that followed was long, dreary days of sus-pense for both Donna and Dale. Dale's interests was with Donna's there, the same as it always was with everything.

The injured outlaw tossed and talked and fought, and there was very few spells in them days that he rested or was anywheres near his right senses. Donna couldn't begin to leave the house, but she didn't have to worry about her riding now, because the day after the doctor came, the cowboy she'd sent after him had come back, made his camp by the corrals, and took it onto himself to do the riding, remarking that there was a lot of Scissor stock close around anyhow, and he had to shove them off.

For the first time in over a year Donna got to put on a house dress and slippers again, but she didn't enjoy 'em much—she'd just as soon be out riding if only everything was all right.

The outlaw went from low to lower, till for a spell it looked like he had joined his kind in other worlds. Dale and Donna stared at one another, hardly breathing, and right then it seemed like whatever that man had done would surely be forgiven by all.

Dale made a motion for Donna to cover his face with the sheet, but she didn't move—she couldn't make herself do what Dale asked of her, not just yet. Dale started to wheel himself away, like as if all was over, and he wanted her to leave too, but she held him and stared at the man in the bed. She thought she'd seen him breathe, once; and sure enough, as she reached for the hunting knife that she'd put away with the outlaw's gun belt, and held the shining blade over his mouth, she seen that it showed moisture. He was coming back to life.

With the strong constitution of the outlaw, living like a wolf as he had, it didn't take long, not more than a day, for him to get good use of his senses. He stared at the wall around him, at Donna, and at Dale, mostly at Dale and the wheel chair he was setting in; then he'd stare at Donna some more. But he was still like a wolf as he stared, some wild animal that'd got used to one way of living and couldn't understand the other.

Next day he started to talk. "What did you do this for?" he asked her. "To see me get in jail?" He couldn't understand why anybody should be good to him.

Donna hushed him up, saying he shouldn't speak or even try to for awhile. He didn't see why he shouldn't think; he kept quiet, and thought, and stared. Dale didn't come and see him no more. Donna figgered it best for him not to, so while he layed staring at the ceiling, the outlaw done plenty of thinking, thoughts that run into one another and left him wondering.

On the third day he got so he could turn his head. The door from the leanto that was his room opened into the kitchen; he could look straight through from there plumb down into the corrals, and there his gaze went the oftenest, sometimes leaving a kink in his neck.

It was early spring, and from dawn till dark his door and the kitchen door was always open, always excepting one day. His door was closed then for a spell, and closed in a way that made him look for his gun-belt, but it wasn't there, and he couldn't even raise his head to look for it.

In a few minutes he heard boot-heels on the porch, and the jingling of spur-rowels, then men's voices, and Donna's.

"Won't you come in?" she was saying.

The men came in, and after a spell, as the one of them started talking, the outlaw was sure of his first suspicions. It was the sheriff and a couple of deputies. The jig was up now, sure enough.

"Well, Dale, how are you these days?" asked the sheriff, neighborly-like. Sheriff Lander was always neighborly, too neighborly for the outlaws.

"Pretty fair," says Dale, "outside of feeling so daggone useless."

"Yeh, I have a hunch of how hard that must be on you. You've always been such an active cuss. But you lack sense, Dale; you should never ride a bronc', once you tie the matrimonial knot; you should turn that work over to other young fellers that's got no responsibilities." He kept quiet for a spell while he sized Dale up; then he asked: "Is there any chance of you recovering from this affliction?"

"I don't know for sure, but I'm told there's a specialist on the coast who could fix me up good as new."

"Well, what the samhill is keeping you here, then?"

Dale grinned. "The usual thing, Sheriff," he says, "the thing most folks are scarce of—money. It'd cost me a thousand dollars to get worked on, and till I get the mortgage settled on my cattle and holdings here, I won't be able to budge."

"I wish I *had* a thousand dollars," says the sheriff.

"So do I," says Dale.

The sheriff squinted at him a second and went on: "I know where there's *two* thousand dollars running around loose," he says, "if I could get my hands on him."

"Him?"

"Yes, him—that outlaw I'm on the trail of now." Dale never blinked an eyelash, and Donna, being already busy at the stove, went on doing just that. "All together," the sheriff went on, "from the stock associations, other associations, and individuals, there's a two-thousand-dollar reward put up for this *hombre*. I pretty near had him a couple of weeks ago too, but he 'brushed' on me. I shot at him a few times, but I don't think I hit him. He'd just caught himself a fresh horse when I jumped him; mine was all in, and I had to turn back. Ain't seen or heard of him since, and I expect he's away down in Mexico by now, but being as I'm always on the go after some-body or other, I'll run across him some day again."

The sheriff and his men stayed for the noon meal. Donna kept busy with the dishes and platters and hardly glanced at Dale all the time they was there, but soon as the jingling of their spurs died down, she layed away the dish she'd been wiping, found a chair, and sat down to stare at Dale. Both stared at one another for quite a spell; then she came to kneel beside him and whispered in his ear: "I just couldn't do it, honey."

Dale looked on straight ahead and nodded, "I savvy, Donna," he says, "and if anybody is to blame, it's me."

There was a mighty puzzled look on the face of the outlaw as Donna brought him a platter of food a few minutes later. He looked at her for a while like as if unbelieving, and he acted like as if he wanted to say something awful bad, but had sort of choked up on it. He et very little, and as the door of his room was left open again, he got another kink in his neck from looking one direction too long. Dale wheeled himself in to see him after a while, and the two talked on about many things, everything but what each wanted to talk about the most, and the nearest the outlaw got to that subject was when he remarked, "I just found out lately," he says, "that a feller can form too strong an opinion on things. Yessir, and when you get to thinking you're all cocksure and right, why, something comes up that shows you you're all wrong."

He was looking through the kitchen toward the corrals next day when a bunch of horses came in to water at the troughs there. One horse attracted his attention, and soon he recognized him as the gray horse he'd been shot off of. He looked at him some more to make sure, and then he called Dale over and asked him:

"What's that gray horse out there, the second one from the left?"

"That's Scorpion. He's the one that crippled me."

"One of *your* horses, then?"

"Yes."

The outlaw stared up at the ceiling for a minute. Then he says: "Hell."

Dale grinned. "I wouldn't of worried if you had run off with him," he says. "I'd never miss him."

"That ain't it with me," says the outlaw. "A horse-thief is a horse-thief, and you folks sure ain't treated me according."

Dale's good hand patted the outlaw on *his* good arm and remarked: "Don't forget what you said yesterday, feller: a man can form too strong an opinion on things."

In the days that followed, the gunsight eyes of the outlaw got a considerable milder. The hard, distrusting glint was gone out of 'em, and instead there appeared a settled and peaceful look, like the kind that might be seen on a man's face when he's picked off a drifting log and hoisted aboard a home-going ship.

A few days went by, and then one morning the door of his room was closed again, like that first time a week or so past, but he didn't look for his gun-belt this time. Something else had drawed his attention, and he begin to reach for it.

In a few minutes, as the time before, he heard boot-heels on the porch, and spurs jingling, then men's voices, and Donna's.

"Won't you come in?" she says. The men came in, and the outlaw, all suspense, listened for the voice of the sheriff. He wasn't disappointed, for soon that official begin talking, and he recognized the voice.

"I just got through with a big job," he was saying, "and now that I got the country sort of peaceable, I'm again making the rounds and looking for that 'Dangerous Dan M'grew.' That's what I call him, 'cause he's took so many names I can't keep track of 'em." Here the sheriff stopped, looked at Donna, then at Dale. "But what stumps me is where could that feller have disappeared to. I never seen tracks evaporate into thin air as his did, and all I can figger is that he sprouted wings, from hereabouts on. . . . You folks ain't happened to seen him, have you?"

Donna was fidgeting with her apron; her face was pale, had been pale ever since the sheriff appeared, for she knowed this question was coming. Dale knowed it too. There was spell of quiet and suspense, and the *tick-tock* of the clock on the shelf was all that could be heard, like a reminder that time was passing and soon an answer would be called for.

As time passed, the sheriff sensed that his question had stirred something. A glance at Donna showed that, and Dale's good hand was fumbling around. Neither was looking at him. He was just about to speak again when a steady voice was heard from behind the closed door of the leanto. That voice though low and quiet, had near the same effect on the listeners as though a gun had been fired and all stared the direction it came.

"All right, Sheriff," the voice had said, and that was all.

Six-shooter in hand, the sheriff kicked the door open and dodged back, but there'd been no use of his doing that, for as he glimpsed at the outlaw he seen that his hands and feet was well tied.

He looked at him in surprise, then turned to Donna. "Well, by golly," he says, "I've sure got hand it to you, Mrs. Maxwell."

"He's been sick," was all Donna said, but as she later looked in at the man, she was also surprised, for she seen how, with the cords of the curtains in his room, the outlaw had tied himself in a way that he couldn't untie. Half-hitches are easy slipped on, but impossible to slip off if they're put on right.

Bedding was piled in a buckboard that afternoon, and all straightened by Donna's hands. The outlaw was carefully layed on that and made comfortable, and as the sheriff and his deputies busied themselves hooking up the borrowed team on the rig, Donna managed to edge near the outlaw, to sort of cheer him up. But there was already a mighty pleased smile on his face, like that of a man who, after being lost and wandering, has at last stumbled on a good, plain trail, a trail that leads to a shining light.

"After I've squared up," he said, as he put out his good hand, "my tracks won't be scattered no more. They'll just be sort of narrow and straight, and going up. But," he went on, "I expect it'll be some time before I make any more tracks, straight or scattered."

The sheriff was hooking up the last tug, and as was his way, he made it his business to hear that last, to which he remarked:

"You can never tell, young feller. The law can be made lenient or severe, and we got a judge in our office that savvies law, but he savvies men the most."

Then, seeing his prisoner was comfortable, he climbs on the seat of the buckboard and started the team.

The first twenty miles of the trip was rough, and very seldom could the team be put to a trot in that distance. The sheriff was busy watching the road, and the prisoner just as busy bracing himself for the jars that couldn't be avoided. Hardly no talk went between the two, only such as, "How're you making it?" from the sheriff, and "All right," from the prisoner. It was away late in the afternoon when there was any change in that conversation, that was as they was going along a smoother piece of road, then the prisoner started to say.

"About that reward, Sheriff——"

"Yes," the sheriff interrupted. "Donna and Dale are going to get that."

But neither Donna nor Dale was thinking of that reward as the two sat on the porch that evening; neither thought how, with that money, Dale could be attended to, and the interest paid on the mortgage. All Dale was doing right then was watching Donna, and Donna was looking at the tracks the buckboard had left, and on her face was sort of half sad and then hopeful expression. Another one of her boys had gone, but with his going, there was no more scattered tracks. Them he left behind was straight and narrow.

XI

FOLKS WEST

The first time I set eyes on this horse I call Chinook was at my ranch one morning and inside my own corrals. A cowboy working for me had gone to visit his brother and brought this sorel horse back with him, and it didn't take me long to spot him amongst my horses, he looked like some dandy horse. There was plain saddle marks on his round back and his head and action showed the wisdom of an old cowboy. That pony had seen and handled many a herd.

It was along noon when I got to speaking to the cowboy about him. The horse belonged to his brother, who was a cowboy too. That brother had been born and raised on the range and got his education from the hills and the men he rode with. He was a good hand with both cattle and horses, and come a time when he begin to hanker for a little range of his own, his own cattle and horses and a solid roof over his head instead of flapping canvas. He saved his money, made his saddle and boots last longer and, late one fall he got a footholt on a good creek and begin cutting logs that'd go to the makings of a two-room house, then a stable and poles for corrals. A cowboy's home.

In time he accumulated a fine little herd of cattle, of the size that made him a good independent living and which he could take care of without having to hire help. He'd ship a couple of carloads of fat cattle every year, store up on a four-horse wagon load of grub, go to breaking a few young horses (Chinook had been one of 'em) and

He was a good hand with both cattle and horses.

spend the winter riding and tending to his cattle, once in a while forking over a little hay to 'em during the worst storms.

He was getting along fine, and then he got married. . . . He didn't marry right and, after the third youngster come and could walk, his wife begin to get lonesome for her folks and town life. The town where her folks lived had two ways of going in and out of, one was the way you came in and the other was the way you went out, there was a general store which was also the post office, a gas station and garage and about a dozen family buildings. Everybody knowed everybody else well and something could always be dug up to gab about. That's the town life she hankered for, and she finally got so she "just couldn't bear it" to live out in the hills and away from it.

Well, thought the cowboy, the kids would soon have to go to school now anyway and so, with a tear in his eye, he sells his little outfit, cattle and all his horses. All but Chinook, he would never sell that horse, he'd said, and so he let his brother, the cowboy who was working for me keep him, he hoped there'd come a time when he could have him again.

But, so far, he hasn't got back to the range. After selling his outfit he took his family, crossed two states to the town where his wife hankered to be and there he changed his riding boots for rubber boots and started at washing automobiles for a living while his wife gabbed around. From then on hard luck begin to camp on his trail and the money he'd got off his ranch and stock begin to dwindle away to pay for doctor bills on the kids and, finally for himself, and one day his brother received a letter from him where he asked if I would buy Chinook, saying that he was sure needing the money and how he knowed the horse would sure have a good home with me. Well, I got to thinking that I would be doing three good turns by buying the horse, one to the horse, one to myself by owning him and one to the busted-down cowboy by helping him, so I paid him the price and the horse was mine.

The last I heard from that cowboy he was still in debt and having a hard time keeping from getting more in debt, he'd got to be a mechanic now in the same garage where he started washing cars.

But I know his heart is sure not with the bolts and nuts and the whole of what goes to make an automobile, he liked his horses too much, and his cattle, and his little country. Maybe his kids make up for that.

This is not an average of what happens when a cowboy marries. There's many a cowboy married and living happy on some spot he picked out for home and range, the wife as a rule is as happy as he is, she can have her pet horses, ride with him, help him take the cattle to the shipping point, ride by his side on the wagon seat when going to town for a new supply of grub and when the fourth of July comes along her and him will both saddle their top horses, lope in and take in a few days' celebrations and shows and the rodeos which is in most western towns at that time. They'll also ride a long ways for winter gatherings that last three and four days at a time.

Mrs. Cowboy can find a plenty to keep her busy and happy at her ranch home, and I've noticed that them who can't are pretty well the kind that's short of vision and with plenty of empty space in the upper story. That kind might come from most anywhere, but are more apt to be from some hick place like I've already described, places where everybody hopes to some day go to the big city and where nobody ever gets to really know the country. They're living neither in town nor the country and so they don't get the benefit of what either would learn them.

It's always a surprise to me to meet people from the sure enough big cities who crave to break away and go to the country, by country

Mrs. Cowboy can find a plenty to keep her busy and happy.

they don't mean a hundred acre farm somewhere, they mean real unplowed wide open country, the kind that many call desolate and where neighbors are miles apart. Most of these people stand high in the best of society and business, they have their summer homes with gardens around and fine big well furnished apartments for the winter when it's hard to get in town. They have all the comforts in the world, many friends, and them is the kind who tell me that as soon as they can tie up their business so they can be free they're coming West, buy a ranch and live as I do. It's not just a dream with 'em either because many have been west and seen our mountains and open country, they're educated to life so they can appreciate what they seen. The wives are just as anxious to come as their husbands, and that shows a heap of contrast as compared to the wife from the hick town who scattered the good independent living and home her cowboy husband had started, "jest so she could be with her (corncob) sassiety." Maybe she's happy now, but I hear the family is living in a tumble down frame shack and that the husband's job is not any too steady.

I noticed that out in the country the people who are the most contented and happy there are them with the best thinking minds and seeing eyes. I know a young couple, both was born and raised on big ranches and both was hard to ship to school when fall come, the boy took his rope with him when he went and the girl took pictures of her top horse. They didn't learn much at school, and when they got married they soon settled on a little outfit of their own and away out in the hills where there was plenty of timber, grass and water. The old folks started 'em out with good cattle and horses, and when I'm saying that them kids was happy I know that I'm putting it pretty weak. Well, they was married about three years when some relative died and left the girl with a fine mansion somewhere in California. With the will was a letter from that relative asking, as a favor, that she would never sell the mansion. It was about middle summer when the news of the inheritance come, and when winter set in the girl and her husband packed up one trunk, left two riders to take care of the ranch and away they went towards sunny California and the mansion. Amongst clothes and other things in the trunk was the latest pictures of the ranch, and the boy didn't forget to throw in his rope.

The mansion didn't disappoint 'em, it was a dandy, made of stone and rambling, with rooms for many servants, guests, and more big rooms for themselves. There was big lawns around, garage, stables and dog kennels, and as the boy said, everything but range to run stock on.

The kids, not having any use for the whole place, made camp in one end of it, hired themselves a housekeeper and her husband and proceeded to make use of the different fine cars that was in the garage. They seen a lot of pretty and strange country, met many good people, went to parties and took on fine shows. All the time and on a table in the big living room was a stack of snapshots that the girl and the boy had took of the ranch and stock, and many times, while sitting by the fireplace, them two would thumb over them pictures, study 'em and pass remarks such as, "I wonder how Pete and Don are getting along, I wish the boys from the camps would write oftener" or "we'll have a pretty good sized branding to do this year." At that the boy would glance at his rope hanging on the corner of a gold framed painting.

With all the comforts of the mansion, the company of many friends and everything the month of March was no more than gone when them two looked at one another, grinned and without saying a word packed the trunk, left the old couple to hold down the place and hit out for their home on the range.

They went to the mansion again the next winter, for just a couple of months and the winter after that they didn't go at all. The girl had leased the big place.

"With that lease money," she'd said, "we can stock up on more cattle and get more range."

I know another couple very different than the one I just told of but with the same liking for the open country of unscarred hills

I wish the boys from the camps would write oftener.

and undammed rivers. This couple is older and have a growed up boy and girl in college. The father was for a long time editor of one of the best known magazines, he's a good author, him and his wife has mingled at gatherings at the White House and with every president from McKinley's time. The princes and kings are his friends, he's been all over the world, seen a lot and had many experiences.

He was fifty years old before he came West, he wouldn't of come then only there was some kind of doings where his presence was wanted. The next year he went of his own free will and took his family with him, and the year after that the whole outfit came out again and he buys a fine big ranch with cattle and horses and all that goes to make up one. Now the family comes out every summer, when I see them on their ranch we talk about horses and cattle and grass and when I happen to see them again in the big city of the East we talk about horses, cattle and grass some more. The father tells me what he plans to do on his ranch next summer and how he hopes he can soon live on it the year around, his wife is as strong for that as he is and she catches him up on any news about the ranch that he might forget to tell and which would interest me. The girl is in love with everything out there and always talks about all of it, and writes to a mighty fine homely cowboy who started a little outfit of his own and just over the hill from the ranch. The boy, he don't remark about any girls yet, when he's in town he describes a new throw he's learned with a rope and when he's on the ranch he *does it* for me. Then I show him another one, and while he's practising that he shows me his horses, again, the little bunch of cattle which his dad turned over to him, and remarks on how fast they increased and how well they looked, specially with his very own brand on their sides.

Years ago, and before the last of the buffalo was killed or put in parks, there was rafts of nobility drift in from Europe and come

There was coachesful of nobility drifted in from Europe and come West to hunt.

West to hunt, some drifted in even after the buffalo was gone, there was still plenty of elk, deer, bear and antelope, and every time a crowd of that nobility came in there was most always some missing when they gathered to go back. The missing ones had took to the hills and stayed there, they'd went to raising cattle or horses and the medals they used to decorate themselves with on big occasions at the palaces went for ornaments on bridles and spurs.

It was only a few years ago when a high standing man of that breed who'd stayed West was notified that if he didn't "come home" he'd lose castle, title and all that went with such. He'd been in Wyoming for more than thirty years, and thinking that over for a spell he buckled on his spurs and went out for a ride amongst some of his cattle and horses, he looked at the snow capped mountains to one side of him and down to the rolling hills below and, he stayed West.

One of the biggest cow outfits in the West and which had ranches scattered from away into Canada, acrost the U.S. and away into Mexico was owned by seventy-six members of the nobility. There's many a big banker, Wall Street broker, oil king who has owned and still own big ranches, and many a son of them has throwed away his coon skin coat along with his college books to pick up a rope and buckle on a pair of shaps.

And the other way around, as some forty-dollar-a-month cowboy got to be governor of his state, or senator and such. Some done mighty well handling stock of the kind that runs on paper tape and which shows no horns, and others done fine in other ways after they dropped their ropes and hung up their saddles. More of 'em could go to the top in other games but few cowboys care to drop their ropes and hang up their saddles.

The open country West teaches a heap more than just plain riding, shooting, roping, few people know that country, and maybe that's a good thing or the big stretches wouldn't be big stretches no more. But when I go to the big cities and see people all up on edge and tired I think of the open country right away. . . . The most of 'em are aching for just that, but they don't know it's that they're aching for . . . they don't know anything about open country and if they was to see it they wouldn't give it a chance to get a holt on 'em, they'd run back to the steel canyons. . . . But a few see it, get to know it, and stay.

Well, I think I'll mosey on over to the corrals now, saddle up Chinook and ride out to see if I can locate a little bunch of cattle of mine that's been missing the last few days. I'm thinking they climbed over the red rims and drifted in the brakes towards the Big Horn.

XII

HORSEFLESH

The horse is an animal, one good starting point in his favor, he eats grass, has a wiry body that's covered with a hide of short hair that's as slick and shiny as silk, he has a clear head and a fine set of brains. The mother will fight till death for her young, she'll fight any animal and anything, anything but man, and sometimes she'll fight him too.

The reason I'm starting with this short description of the horse is so the reader would have an idea of what that animal is. . . . Where most people live nowadays, in the cities, the horse is only something that's fastened to the front end of a dray or garbage wagon. Nobody ever notices him, they'll look past him to the shiny hood of a new make of motor car, or else above him to the skies where the roar of an airplane is heard. The store windows have a lot of attractions too. There is things electrical that'll speak and sing by the hour by just turning a switch, things that'll make toast, coffee and cook a meal without being watched, just turn another switch, even clocks don't have to be wound any more . . . and I wouldn't be surprised if, with all things that's mechanical and machinery and which draws so much interest, people will turn to be machines too. There might come a time when bolts, wheels and springs will be found in men's heads, deferential grease taking the place of mara at the joints and lubricating oil running thru the veins instead of blood.

You take nine out of ten of the kids, and grown ups too, that's born and raised in the big cities and if you was to ask 'em what a

He has a clear head and a fine set of brains.

horse eats they'd be apt to say corned beef and cabbage, they'd hardly know if beef is off an ox or something that is picked off trees in a can.

Even on the farms, there's young fellers that don't know how to milk a cow or drive a team of horses, the cow is milked by machine and the plow is pulled by a tractor.

All these inventions to save time and labor, and these machines of speed that take you where you want to go while you're thinking about it are mighty fine I guess. We're sure doing a lot of things in a hurry and getting there a lot faster than our granddads did, but I sure don't think we're getting any further than our granddads, nor seeing as much, or doing more things and as well. People's blood is turning to oil and burning up for speed.

The proof of the human's craving for animal company is showed by many folks "serving time" in the big cities. You see men and women going along following little dogs, apartment size, and watching their every move the same as if that pet was all that mattered in the world, the nurse might take the child out for the airing but they'll take the dog themselves. That I think sort of explains how close animal ties up with human life.

What instinct is it that makes a kid pick up a skinny and homely pup and cry to his mother to let him keep him? . . . The kid might not know what a dog is good for, how to take care of him or feed him, but he wants him and wants him bad. . . . And how many kids or grown ups would like to have a pony or a horse, just to have him, keep him and so as to touch his hide once in a while and be near him.

A person that hasn't got a soft spot or craving for some kind of animal is either not human or else is plum ignorant of what an animal is. The first kind is scarce and the last kind is getting numerous.

I was in a few of the big cities of the East last fall and mixed with some gatherings at clubs and other places where I was asked to stand up and say "howdy" and follow that up with a few words. At one place where I stood up and done my best to make my few words good was a gathering of about five hundred school children from sixteen-years-olds on up to eighteen. They was a bright looking bunch of kids and they savvied a lot, they knowed how an airplane was made and many had often been up in one, most of 'em came to school with the folks' car and they could drive it well. They knowed all about Greece, Egypt and European points.—When I got thru with my few words one of the kids edges towards me and asks, "Where is Montana, isn't it just north of Minneapolis?" I had a Harvard man who's been all over the world, excepting his own country, ask me a worse one than that.

While I was talking to the kids it came to my mind to ask if any of 'em knowed how come the horse to be in our country, who brought the first ones over and so on, and I was surprised to see that in all that bunch only one raised a hand, that one wasn't so sure of himself either. All he said was that a Spaniard brought the first horses over, he didn't know how long ago nor what the name of the Spaniard was. The other kids, and even the teachers, seemed surprised to learn that our first horses had been brought in from a foreign country, they thought he'd been here all the time.

I don't know myself where I learned that the first horses had been brought over on a boat from Spain, by Cortez and over four or five hundred years ago but it seems to me like I knowed that when I was born. Like the history of the West, that was handed to me from old timers as I growed up, the same as it was handed to them as they growed up from other old timers, and that way all the way back and in many languages to the time of Cortez.

From what I remember hearing off and on and around the cow camps, these horses was Arabians, there was about seventeen head to start with, they accumulated, a few would get away now and again and hit for the hills where, as time went on, them few accumulated some more and all got as wild as antelopes. That was the start of our western horses which got to be called mustangs or wild horses. Them wild horses spread all along the west from Mexico to Oregon, and even tho there's been other imported breeds mixed in with 'em there's many a wild horse still shows strains of the Arabian in him, specially in the Southwest. And to day, with most everybody gone mechanic, there's still thousands of wild horses in my country West.

There's not much use for the horse any more, only out on the range, the automobile and tractors has took his place pretty well. Everybody's hands are broke to steering wheels and wrenches and wouldn't know how to use lines or reins. Most everybody's forgot, or never learned what the horse has done before motors came in. It was him and the oxen that hauled the first families west and packed

There's not much use for the horse any more.

WILL JAMES
. III ~ 21.

man on his galded back while that man was looking for gold, or hunting and trapping and finding a place where he could build a cabin for himself and family. The horse had saved many a man's scalp too from the raiding Indians.

I don't blame anybody for sort of forgetting the horse, it's as a feller says to me one time "We all have to keep up with the times." True enough, but I'll bet my ranch against a doughnut that if I could gather a few million horses about the size of one of these little muff dogs that I sure wouldn't have no trouble finding homes for 'em.

A few would get away now and again and hit for the hills.

Anybody that likes a dog would like a horse.

With me, I like all animals, excepting one kind and I'll come to that one kind some other time, but above all animals I like the horse best. Maybe that's because I was born and raised, lived and still live where that animal is seldom further than a rope's length away from me. I've knowed and rode all kinds of horses in all parts of the range country, some was mean ones that handed me hard knocks, some was just good mean ones, and many was good ones. I made my living for many years while setting in the middle of one after another such animal and handling the big herds of cattle. I rode fifty-two head of wild and unbroke horses in one day on inspection for the French government who'd sent men west to buy horses, about forty of the horses done their best to buck me off and, towards the last, a few of 'em did.

What I like about the horse is how independent he naturally is. On that account, people that don't know him say he has no brains and claim that a dog has a lot more, that's because they know more about dogs. Myself, I think that both have the same amount of brains, only different kinds. The horse don't care a daggone if you like him or not so long as you don't abuse him, where the dog will look for favors, lick your hand and want to be fussed over. The horse is in the stable or out on grass while the dog is at your feet, you'll talk to a dog about a hundred times more than you do to a horse and another thing is that the horse don't depend on you for a living, he'll do fine if he's free, where the dog pretty well looks to you handing him a platter of bones. The dog is your company, your pet, while the horse is just an animal to pull a wagon or a plow or saddle up and lope out on.

In a way I'm mighty glad that so many kinds of machines and motors has come to take the place of the horse. I miss seeing him, when I'm in town, but the few of his kind that I see, being jerked at

What I like about a horse is how independent he naturally is.

the bit like no feeling was there and by some gink with narrow brain space, I sometimes get so I could hug a truck for taking the place of at least two and more horses. You might hurt a motor and ruin it by running it without oil or grease but that's just hurting cold steel and iron, and it will quit, but work a horse on short feeds of hay and grain and you're hurting flesh with nerves of feeling thru it the same as you and me have. The motor will quit but the horse will keep on going even tho he's sick, hungry, tired, iron shoes pinching his feet and bad teeth hurting him.

On my ranch I have three times more horses than I really need. Consequences is, with always fresh ones to change to, none ever get very tired, there's no sore backs nor sore shoulders, and no pinching shoes because none of my horses are ever shod. When one gets a little sore footed another one takes his place. My horses are out in the hills and tall grass the year around and live the same free life as the mustang does, no hard stable floors for them to stand on day in and day out.

I keep on an average of ten head of saddle horses in my private string, with my writing and drawing taking a lot of my time nowdays I have use for only about one or two. Strangers sometimes ask me what do I do with all them horses and that strikes me as tho some people can't picture a horse unless he's pulling or packing something, as tho he ought to earn his right to live. I have some old horses that haven't been rode for a couple of years, they're sound and good yet, they're eating a lot of grass that would feed more cattle, I could sell the horses, spend the money and save that grass but I'd rather keep the old horses, even if just to look at.

So, with horses, cattle and other stock that's all around me and which ever way I look I know I'll never learn to regulate the pulse of a motor, the thumping of my horse's heartbeats as he spots a bunch of mustangs will always be good enough for me.

And, as I happen to look out my cabin window right now I see one of my top horses that I call Big-Enough nibbling at the buds of a young cottonwood tree I just had planted, he ain't got much to do but eat and stay fat and get into mischief, I'll have to go out and chase him away so he won't kill that tree.

THE END